MW00617948

PENGUIN LIFE

I DECIDED TO LIVE AS ME

Kim Suhyun is a writer and illustrator based in Seoul. She loves drawing, so in college she studied design. She describes herself as "thoughtful but not too serious, lighthearted but not shallow." Her books have sold more than two million copies in Korea, and *I Decided to Live as Me* is being published around the world in more than a dozen languages.

Anton Hur was a finalist for the National Book Award for Translated Literature and the International Booker Prize for his translation of *Cursed Bunny* by Bora Chung and has also translated *I Want to Die but I Want to Eat Tteokbokki* by Baek Sehee and co-translated *Beyond the Story* by BTS. He is the author of the novel *Toward Eternity*.

I DECIDED TO LIVE AS ME

*An Illustrated Checklist for How to
Stop Comparing Yourself to Others
So You Can Learn to Love Yourself*

Kim Suhyun

Translated by Anton Hur

life

PENGUIN BOOKS
An imprint of Penguin Random House LLC
penguinrandomhouse.com

A Penguin Life Book

Originally published in Korean as 나는 나로 살기로 했다 by Clayhouse Inc.,
Paju-si, Gyeonggi-do, South Korea.

Published with the support of Literature Translation Institute of Korea (LTI Korea).

LIBRARY OF CONGRESS CATALOGING-IN-PUBLICATION DATA
Names: Kim, Su-hyŏn (Writer), author, illustrator. | Hur, Anton, translator.
Title: I decided to live as me: an illustrated checklist for how to stop comparing yourself
to others so you can learn to love yourself / Kim Suhyun; translated by Anton Hur.
Other titles: Na nŭn na ro salgi ro haetta. English Description: New York: Penguin Books, an
imprint of Penguin Random House LLC, [2024] | "Originally published in Korean as 나는 나로
살기로 했다 by Clayhouse Inc., Paju-si, Gyeonggi-do, South Korea." | Translated from the
Korean. | Identifiers: LCCN 2024031196 (print) | LCCN 2024031197 (ebook) | ISBN
9780143138228 (board) | ISBN 9780593512388 (ebook)
Subjects: LCSH: Conduct of life. | Self-realization. | Self-esteem.
Classification: LCC BJ1588.K6 K57 2024 (print) | LCC BJ1588.K6 (ebook) |
DDC 158.1—dc23/eng/20240822
LC record available at https://lccn.loc.gov/2024031196
LC ebook record available at https://lccn.loc.gov/2024031197

Printed in the United States of America
1st Printing

Designed by Nerylsa Dijol

Time passes and everything changes
but you will always be yourself.

CONTENTS ♠♠

PART SIX

**CHECKLIST FOR
A GOOD AND
MEANINGFUL LIFE**

PREFACE

It's been five years since the first Korean publication of *I Decided to Live as Me*. One of the questions I've received most is "What made you write this book?" Well, I used to have a kind of checklist for life: go to college, get a good job, get married, buy an apartment, have children, and become an adult of refined taste with a comfortable lifestyle. To live like everybody else, in other words, or like everybody was watching.

But oddly enough (for reasons I understand all too well now), this never came to fruition. Without being able to check off the first few boxes, I couldn't move on to the later ones. My failure to complete my life's checklist made me feel so ashamed of myself.

What had I done wrong? Should I have listened to the world more, concentrated more, forced myself to work harder? Or should I have been a different kind of person altogether?

But as I kept questioning myself, I suddenly had a thought: *What if that's not it?*

The moment I thought, *What if it's not my fault?*, I began to notice the problems in our society. The moment I thought, *What if my ideal life isn't the only answer?*, I began searching for other answers. The moment I thought, *What if the majority is wrong?*, I gained the courage to live the writer's life.

This book started with the idea *What if that's not it?* and with all the questions and answers that followed.

From that one question I learned many answers and found the strength to let go of the lies surrounding my life and accept myself for who I was. It was such a liberating experience that I wanted to share it with readers.

Still, I hope this book doesn't make you feel as if I'm trying to force something on you. All I ask is that you question things like I started to do, and take a step away from our societal conventions and try to find your own answers.

On the days I'd work on the book, I'd walk home in the evening with a feeling of lightness, a feeling so refreshing that I still think about it from time to time.

I hope this book helps you achieve that feeling. Five years on, I am still cheering for all of you on your life's journey. Good luck, everyone, and keep on living well.

Kim Suhyun

INTRODUCTION

Looking back, I always wanted to know the "why." Whenever my teachers at school asked me to do something, I would respond, "Why?" They thought I was being difficult, but I was asking out of genuine curiosity. I couldn't help but ask questions and seek answers.

Then I became an adult, and I began to feel small and pathetic. A shadow of a person, with nothing to call my own and no real accomplishments to my name. How on Earth did I end up like this?

I wondered where I had gone wrong. Did I choose the wrong major? Should I have studied harder? Should I have stuck with certain jobs instead of quitting them? No matter how hard I thought, I couldn't really point to anything I'd done wrong.

I'd made a few mistakes and lacked direction, but wasn't all that just part of growing up? Just as I had always wanted to know why, as a student, I wanted to figure out why I felt pathetic despite not having done anything wrong.

I turned to books, not because reading was a hobby but because I wanted answers. Why did I feel so insignificant? Why wasn't I enough? Why was I such a nothing?

At the end of the day, I came to the conclusion that even if the world doesn't value me, I have to have self-respect and live confidently as me. This book delves into the reasons why I felt pathetic and my reactions to all the things that made me feel that way.

Throughout my career, the things I've written may have helped a reader or two, even if for only a moment. But what I've really wanted to do is create a source of healing and support that can stay with them for longer.

I want to tell those of you who, like me, keep blaming yourselves when you are not at fault: it's not your fault.

It is all right to live as you.

I DECIDED TO
LIVE AS ME

GOAL

For an ordinary person
to let go of what they are not,
to endure the judgment of others,
and to still live exactly as they are.

PART ONE

Checklist for a Life
That Respects Who You Are

Medicine, law, business, engineering—these are noble
pursuits, and necessary to sustain life.
But poetry, beauty, romance, love—these are what
we stay alive for.

—*DEAD POETS SOCIETY*

☑ DO NOT BE POLITE TO THOSE WHO ARE NOT POLITE TO YOU

Right out of college I did an internship. That first boss I had, in my first job ever, treated me like . . . a servant? She bullied me, basically. Asking me to move by four inches the monitor that was right in front of her, cursing me out for the smallest mistake. It was my first corporate job, and with an offer of full-time employment on the line, I was torn over whether to stay or go. Every day on that job hammered home the fact that *Homo internus* was the lowest being on the corporate food chain.

Several years after I finished the internship, I was lying in bed when I was suddenly consumed with rage by that memory.

It was less her behavior that I couldn't stand and more the fact that I just put up with it. It wasn't like she was all-powerful, but I didn't say a word to her in my defense, and that just encouraged her to act worse.

This isn't the same thing, but it is said that those tortured for their involvement in South Korea's democracy movement are hurt most not by the physical pain they suffered but by their degrading attempts to assuage their torturers.

This may not be our fault, but the truly fatal blow to our dignity isn't the mistreatment we endure but how humiliatingly we respond to it.

To those who are not kind to you, who do not respect you—don't bother being polite to them in return. Even in demeaning situations, you can at least hold on to some of your dignity.

∧∧∧∧∧∧∧∧∧∧∧∧∧∧∧∧∧∧∧∧∧∧∧∧

EVEN IF WE CAN'T CHANGE THE SITUATION,

WE NEED TO PUSH BACK A LITTLE TO PROTECT

OUR DIGNITY FROM THE WORST KIND OF PEOPLE.

∧∧∧∧∧∧∧∧∧∧∧∧∧∧∧∧∧∧∧∧∧∧∧∧

What gives bullies strength isn't their position, but the helpless politeness of the bullied.

☑ DON'T GO OUT OF
YOUR WAY TO BE MISERABLE

When I first entered the new world that was Instagram, my feed randomly showed me a woman whose breasts were so large that they practically covered her torso. Her posts oozed luxury. She was pretty, thin, expensively dressed, and always traveling. But what came as a shock wasn't her lavish lifestyle but her number of followers.

Why were so many people obsessed with her? Looking through her photos made me feel sad about the tasty convenience-store kimbab I had that morning and the cute, spangled bag I "scored" for only 8,900 won.

Social media makes it too easy to snoop on others and their perfect lives.

But is such voyeurism truly free? In his book *Shake It Off! Build Emotional Strength for Daily Happiness*, Rafael Santandreu argues that snooping on others' lives and comparing them to our own is the easiest way to make ourselves miserable.

We might look at someone's social media profile out of curiosity and pay the price for it with misery. There is nothing to be gained from this. Your energy and curiosity are better spent on taking care of yourself.

So be someone's friend, not a member of their audience.

Compared to the shallow summary of their lives through photos, the reality of our own experiences is surely more precious.

^^^^^^^^^^^^^^^^^^^^^^^^^^

DON'T GO OUT OF YOUR WAY

TO MAKE YOURSELF MISERABLE.

^^^^^^^^^^^^^^^^^^^^^^^^^^

Envy doesn't make you unhappy; forgetting what you already have does.

Envy is destructive because it makes what you already have seem worthless.

☑ DON'T GET HURT BY THOSE WHO ARE JUST PASSING THROUGH YOUR LIFE

Something I've begun to realize as I get older is that even people you really want to see have trouble making time for you. To say nothing of those you dislike or don't get along with—like my high school classmate Eunkyung or Mr. Park in accounting. In the end, they're all people who are just passing through.

But we still allow ourselves to get hurt when people say they can't meet up because they're too busy with work, or when they criticize us but say they're doing so out of concern, disguising insults as questions.

It's not only things like spending twice your paycheck on a luxury bag or obsessing over a celebrity's lifestyle that are a waste of your time. Devoting your mental energy to those who are only passing through your life is also a waste.

Don't spend your energy on some boss you won't even remember after you quit or a relative you see only occasionally or some office gossip who insults you with a smile or a colleague who is obviously scheming against you or anyone else who means nothing to you.

**EXASPERATING, INFURIATING, AND HATEFUL
AS SOME PEOPLE ARE, IN THE END THEY'RE JUST
PASSING THROUGH YOUR LIFE.**

☑ GET RID OF NUMBERS IN YOUR LIFE

From a meme about what qualifies someone as middle class around the world:

ENGLAND (ACCORDING TO A STUDY BY THE UNIVERSITY OF OXFORD):

- ○ Has their own convictions and opinions
- ○ Is not foolishly stubborn
- ○ Protects the weak and stands up to the strong
- ○ Readily battles injustice, inequality, and illegality

FRANCE (ACCORDING TO PRESIDENT POMPIDOU'S "QUALITY OF LIFE" STANDARDS):

- ○ Speaks at least one foreign language and has a global outlook
- ○ Can cook at least one dish well enough to serve to others
- ○ Does volunteer work
- ○ Can scold the children of others like one's own

KOREA (ACCORDING TO A SURVEY FROM AN EMPLOYMENT INFORMATION WEBSITE):

- ○ Can afford a three-bedroom apartment without loans
- ○ Has an income of at least 5 million won a month
- ○ Has a midsized sedan or better

- ⭘ Has 100 million won in the bank
- ⭘ Takes several overseas trips a year

What do the Korean standards include that the UK's and France's don't?

Numbers.

Once when I was surfing the web, I came across an ad offering to tell me my "marriage score." It wasn't for a fortune-telling site like I initially thought but for a marriage broker. You input your age, height, weight, net worth, income, and more to be graded like beef at a market. Can any other AI be more truly Korean?

We love assigning numbers to things so much that we naturally accept assigning numbers to ourselves.

In this life-in-numbers, we obsess over having the right numbers on our résumés, determine who's worth our time by how big their house is, and during strikes or protests, promote not the underlying issues but how much they cost. When only numbers are sought, true value is forgotten.

The thing about numbers is they're so easy to compare. You can't really compare a circle to a triangle, but anyone can measure 1 against 2. In the end, a life of numbers is all about comparing ourselves to and ranking ourselves against one another.

In this game, we're anxious we won't measure up, so we constantly check our position in the rankings. But can everything in life be measured through numbers?

An IQ score is not a measure of wisdom, the number of friends we have doesn't say anything about the depths of our friendships, the number of rooms in someone's house doesn't guarantee a happy family, and someone's yearly income doesn't reflect their integrity.

True value cannot be measured in numbers. If you want to be your own person rather than someone who is merely "superior" to others, you must eliminate numbers from your life.

^^^^^^^^^^^^^^^^^^^^^^^^^

WHAT IS TRULY IMPORTANT IN LIFE

CANNOT BE EXPRESSED IN NUMBERS.

^^^^^^^^^^^^^^^^^^^^^^^^^

Who are you without your numbers?

* The Test of English for International Communication (TOEIC) is an English-language proficiency test used around the world by companies in their hiring processes.

☑ DON'T BE AFFECTED
BY WHAT OTHERS SAY

Jungmi, my reader and friend through social media, is a lovely and warm person. She has an affectionate boyfriend whom she often posts about, and their love has rekindled my dying faith in relationships. But then some stranger posted a comment saying she should "stop with all the cuddly content," that there were people who weren't as fortunate as she was.

Of course there are those who post too much on social media—but I assure you, she wasn't one of them. The comment caused her to doubt herself. But the fault lay with the commenter, who hadn't dealt with their own issues.

There will always be people who misread us and attack us based on their own twisted interpretations. Those who used to be confined to the comments sections of online publications now roam freely in the comments sections of social media.

A word of advice about how to deal with such people: First, when someone criticizes you, keep in mind that this is only an individual's opinion—and the individual in question is not exactly King Solomon or Sigmund Freud.

Second, rather than feel angry or sad, determine whether there's any truth to the criticism. If there is, then think of it as an opportunity for you to improve. And if it's something stemming from the person's own issues, then regard it as just the barking of a dog. And if the dog continues to bark? Don't just listen to it, take action against it.

For what? Slander? No. Excessive noisemaking.

Just show this page to online trolls.
Note: I know you are, but what am I?

☑ DON'T LIVE A LIFE OF INSULTS

I recently saw an online post filled with misspellings. Immediately people flooded the comments with the word "geukhyeom," which is short for "extremely disgusting." I couldn't understand what was so disgusting about it. It wasn't as if a few misspellings were a personal insult hurled at King Sejong, inventor of the Hangul alphabet. Were the person's misspellings worthy of such disgust?

We have come to hate one another too easily.

This recent rise in hatred is often attributed to the breakdown of the middle class. Presumably, those who feel threatened will threaten others in order to retain their status. But that isn't all. The hate is too wide and indiscriminate to stem from just that. I'm called a kimchi bitch solely for existing as a Korean woman, a job leech if I marry but continue in my job instead of handing it over to some man, a mom parasite if I bring a child out in public spaces, or a know-it-all if I try to explain something.

The author Kim Chanho says that people demean others to overcome the emptiness they feel in a world where being good enough is never enough.

These insults come from a compulsion to feel superior, to compensate for a sense of inferiority, and to validate one's existence. How pathetic is that?

Haters unite in solidarity, cover for one another's inadequacies, and reinforce their twisted view of the world. Those who are targeted by their hate mirror it back to them. This results in an endless contest to determine who is the most hateful of all.

But in the end, is there really any satisfaction in confirming how hateful we all are? All this does is make us more nervous and on edge.

I FIRMLY BELIEVE THAT IN A WORLD WHERE PEOPLE DO NOTHING BUT ATTACK ONE ANOTHER, NO ONE CAN EVER BE HAPPY.

✦

If you don't wipe the grease spot off your own camera lens, the whole world will be smudged forever.

In a department store elevator, a baby being carried by her mother burst into tears. Alarmed, the mother told the baby that she must not cry. She glanced at me, and I said to her, "It's all right." What I meant was, "I will not judge you."

Really, it's all right.

It's all right.

☑ DO NOT MAKE EXCUSES FOR YOURSELF

I once heard about a man who graduated from a good school but whose history of student activism prevented him from getting a job. He hated capitalism for it and refused to work in such an unfair system. Eventually he stopped looking for a job entirely, and his mother, who was a housekeeper, supported them both.

Clearly, the man's logic was flawed. He criticized capitalism for exploiting its workers, but he exploited the work of his own mother. Those around him pitied his mother and couldn't understand why he wouldn't even try to work. What had made him into such a hypocrite?

I suspect he had high hopes for himself, having graduated from such a good school. He must've felt frustrated and helpless in the face of all the prejudice against him for having been a student activist. His failure to fulfill society's expectations of him must've been a blow to his self-esteem.

Humiliation and worthlessness are among the hardest feelings to deal with. Many of those who suffer from them hide behind cynicism and blame others to protect themselves.

The problem is that their excuses aren't enough to defend them. Their excuses don't fool even themselves. Despite their attempts to hide their helplessness and shame, they continue to fester underneath it all.

As many have said, the opposite of love isn't hate or rage but indifference. Similarly, the opposite of living isn't death or aging—it's delusion. Being deluded makes people deny reality and live a pretend existence.

The man avoided reality for a long time. Maybe he thought it easier to act as a martyr of resistance rather than confront his shame. Maybe he was afraid our judgmental world would hurt him.

But he shouldn't have wasted his life dwelling on what might have been. Whatever the reasons for his resentments, he should've rid himself of them and taken stock of himself.

He should feel proud of his college days when he tried to make a better world and accept that some things had not come to pass. What he should really feel ashamed of isn't his lack of success but that he has done nothing except make excuses for himself.

Even if this wasn't the future he hoped for, and even if he feels embarrassed, he must let go of his excuses and confront his true self.

^^^^^^^^^^^^^^^^^^^^^^^^^^^

**THE MOST IMPORTANT THING IS THAT AFTER
CONFRONTING YOURSELF, A NEW BEGINNING AWAITS.**

^^^^^^^^^^^^^^^^^^^^^^^^^^^

"I'm so pathetic."
Attacking inward

"No, it's not my fault."
Attacking outward

The important thing is to free yourself from resentment.

☑ REMEMBER THAT NO ONE'S LIFE IS PERFECT

In the ninth grade, a boy once said to me, "You seem like you have an **easy** life." I guess he was taken in by my cheerful and friendly appearance. But deep down, I had a lot of adolescent angst and fought constantly with my parents. And I was jealous of another pretty and popular classmate, whose life looked absolutely perfect. Years later, this very classmate confided in me that ninth grade had been her hardest year. Fascinating—both the boy and I had wrongly judged a person in the same way. We had believed others' lives were perfect simply because they seemed to have what we lacked.

How well can we really know someone? In the last episode of the drama *Age of Youth* (written by Park Yeon-seon), envious gossip surrounds Jin-myung as she leaves for China for a month: "I wish that were me," "I wish I was born rich." But the truth is that Jin-myung had waited six years for her comatose brother to die before scraping together her meager savings to go overseas.

We judge a person by how they appear on the outside, but what we **see** of them is only the tip of the iceberg—just as what others see of us is only a small part of who we are. This applies especially to personal hardships, which absolutely everyone has but others rarely see.

Always remind yourself that no one's life is perfect. Sometimes this reminder alone is enough of a consolation.

✦

Having seen me on my computer, a friend sent me this message: *You're always working so hard, you're an inspiration.* All I had been doing was tracking a package delivery.

The Perspective of Wounds

My own wounds appear larger than others'.

☑ BE PERFECTLY CONTENT WITH BEING ORDINARY

Whenever I rode in a car as a little girl, I thought the sun followed me everywhere. I also expected to become a magical superhero like Sailor Moon when I grew up. If I continued to think like that as an adult, I would probably be diagnosed as delusional. Yet for a long time I assumed that even if I didn't quite become a superhero and save the world from evil, I would eventually grow up to be a special person.

But I grew up to be ordinary. My life isn't fancy by any means, and lots of things weigh me down. I can't buy everything I want—not by a long shot. And every day is a repetition of the previous one, proceeding straight down the narrow track that is my life.

The point when you realize you've become another ordinary adult—in other words, when you let go of your childhood dreams—is the very point when your adult adolescence begins.

This can be a sad, bitter moment, but perhaps it is every adult's duty to shrug off their childhood fantasies and create a realistic life for themselves.

I may never become Sailor Moon and save the world or have lunch with Warren Buffett or become a professor at the Sorbonne.

And my former classmates may never turn green with envy at the thought of me, and my family may never speak grandly of me as someone who brings honor to our household.

But I have books I want to write and things I want to learn about. I want to spend time with my family, learn to swim and spend hours by the sea, and meet new people from different walks of life who will expand my worldview.

There are many limitations on my life and few guarantees—besides death and taxes, of course—but even an ordinary life isn't completely without promise.

Your adult adolescence will end when you accept the ordinary nature of your life and find what is fulfilling within it.

∧∧∧∧∧∧∧∧∧∧∧∧∧∧∧∧∧∧∧∧∧∧∧∧

ONLY IN ACHIEVING ACCEPTANCE

CAN ONE TRULY BECOME AN ADULT.

∧∧∧∧∧∧∧∧∧∧∧∧∧∧∧∧∧∧∧∧∧∧∧∧

Being special doesn't come from being superior but from being yourself.

✅ DON'T ALLOW ANYONE TO JUDGE YOU

My friend once went on a blind date and was asked if she liked golf or horseback riding. This wasn't so much an expression of interest in her hobbies as an interrogation of her economic class.

To gauge someone's finances isn't always a bad thing—I'm hardly innocent of this myself. But there's a difference between gathering information for a life decision and pounding the calculator in someone's face, reducing their worth to numbers.

This friend also told me about a man who ghosted her after he learned where she lived, and a man who spent their only date trying to figure out what her parents did for a living. They made her feel like she had to pass a test, and she became anxious about being judged. But on the other hand, did she have to care about their judgment?

I personally don't care how rich someone is. People who like to calculate such things seem narrow-minded and pretentious to me, not sexy. Definitely not anyone I'd want to get hitched to.

I may be less than adequate to them. But to me, so are they.

What I want is someone similar to me—I mean, two can play at this judgment game. So who cares if someone tries to see if I measure up financially?

What a joke. I reject all of you back, you rejects.

WHO CARES?
Didn't ask, don't care.

☑ DON'T BE MODEST TO THE POINT OF LOW SELF-ESTEEM

After I became a published author, my friends would call me Writer Kim, but I would take it as their teasing me—I didn't seriously consider myself a writer. Even though the dictionary definition of writer is someone who writes, the designation always felt awkward when applied to me.

Then I heard a story of a tourist who met a bartender in some European pub. When the bartender introduced himself as a poet, the tourist asked, "Have you published a collection?" The bartender replied, "No, I haven't. I'm a poet because I write poems."

How can I feel so unsure about calling myself a writer even after publishing several books, while someone else who's never published a book can so easily call himself a poet? Personality differences aside, there are also cultural differences. In the West, where individuality and freedom are emphasized, children are taught to think of themselves as special.

In Korea, we emphasize a harmonious society over the personality of the individual, which is why as soon as we enter elementary school, we study a subject called Proper Living—all about how to get along with others.

We are educated away from thinking we are special and from prioritizing our own feelings and instead are told to lower ourselves and pay more attention to the feelings of others.

This is the cultural basis for Koreans' heightened sense of "nunchi"— "reading the room"—and our supposed modesty that comes dangerously close to self-degradation.

And because these values are ingrained in us from a young age, it's second nature for us to use our nunchi and modesty to play down our own qualifications and avoid accusations of being high and mighty for the sake of getting along with others. We are always questioning our worth as individuals. Of course, modesty and consideration for others are virtues. But even virtues, when excessive, overflow into toxicity.

But true virtue is in respecting others, not diminishing ourselves to the point of feeling worthless. If you worry about what others think at the expense of your own feelings, surely there's no virtue in that. Don't exhaust yourself with nunchi and don't be modest to the point of low self-esteem.

^^^^^^^^^^^^^^^^^^^^^^^^^^^

THE PERSON YOU SHOULD RESPECT MOST

IS ALWAYS YOURSELF.

^^^^^^^^^^^^^^^^^^^^^^^^^^^

You need a bit of an ego and a dash of "Screw it—it's my way or the highway!"

☑ SPEAK OUT FOR THE RIGHT TO RESPECT YOURSELF

I read a post on social media about a customer who pointed at a restaurant server and then said to her daughter, "If you don't study hard, you'll end up like her." The server was miffed by this drive-by insult. She was working in a restaurant just for the experience, she said, and was even attending an exclusive university. Then some Chinese guests sat down and, having studied in China, she served them in fluent Mandarin. The customer who'd pointed at her was taken aback.

The comments on the post were mostly critical of the customer. But how different, really, are the server and the customer? The server had taken pains to emphasize that she was not an ordinary worker, just someone working part time for the experience. She was indignant, insisting that she didn't deserve to be treated "like a server." Because she considered herself above those who "didn't study hard."

There's that recent internet craze over motivational quotes: "Do you want to have fun in college or work in a factory?" "Good GPAs order chicken, bad GPAs fry it, and no transcripts deliver it." It reduces working in food delivery or factories to a punishment for laziness and portrays honest labor as degrading. Memes like this show how class discrimination is engraved into our psyches.

The roots of this discrimination run deep. Ancient hierarchies in which the rulers have status and the ruled are devalued, despite our collective reliance on the fruits of workers' labor, have been reborn in modern capitalist society. This dynamic continues to make it difficult to narrow the wage gap between professions, which in turn perpetuates old prejudices.

How exactly does this problem manifest?

I.

It goes way beyond simply violating the basic human right to equality. Children who are constantly reminded of what happens if they don't study will be conditioned to see as legitimate role models only the successful businesspeople on TV dramas.

And many physical laborers actually do face discrimination and harassment at work.

How will those who grew up to expect a life that looks like a K-drama and yet find themselves in roles they had been conditioned to look down on ever be content?

Delusions of future grandeur and systemic discrimination come home to roost in the form of shame at one's own ordinariness. How unacceptable that they should be like *those people*. This becomes self-hatred.

2.

Discrimination against workers takes many forms. Anyone who shrinks from manual labor closes themselves off to some of the joy of learning or the respect for honest work. Such a person studies only because they are anxious and afraid; they are the kind of person who has motivational quotes taped up on their walls. But when one's sole motivation is anxiety or fear, nothing can overcome the resulting fatigue. The harmful pressure a parent puts on their child manifests inside the child as chronic anxiety and exhaustion.

3.

Let's say you get where you want to go. Does it feel like enough? Achievement built on prejudice only begets arrogance. To have high self-regard without true inner strength is like standing on the roof of a skyscraper with no railing: all you can feel is the constant fear that you will fall. And the bigger one's ego, the harder their fall. There was an op-ed about this, saying that when people face adversity, they should seek a soft landing, a better way to fall. But Koreans refuse to come down, and when forced to, we face a terrible reckoning at the bottom.

Life will always have its ups and downs, but to those with internalized prejudices and self-contempt, every down becomes a tragic fall. Discrimination makes those on the receiving end ashamed, and those on the giving end anxious. Ultimately, it helps no one.

If you constantly recharge your anxiety batteries, or you feel shame for living a life far from the one you dreamed of, you have to tell yourself the truth: there are many ways to live a life, and no way of life is wrong.

Live and learn as diligently as you want. But no one has the right to insult someone else for how they live.

^^^^^^^^^^^^^^^^^^^^^^^^^

WE EACH HAVE THE RIGHT TO HAVE

OUR WAY OF LIFE RESPECTED.

^^^^^^^^^^^^^^^^^^^^^^^^^

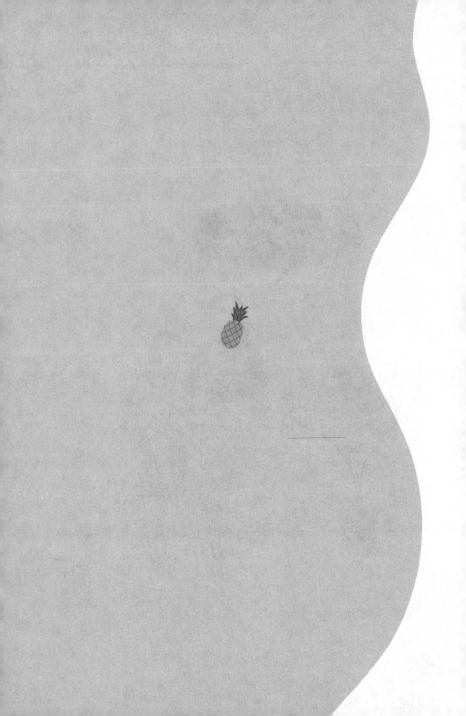

PART TWO

Checklist for
Living as Yourself

Rather be hated for what you are
than loved for what you are not.

—Kurt Cobain

☑ HAVE A STRONG SENSE
OF YOUR SELF-WORTH

The popular philosopher Alain de Botton described adulthood as staking out our place in a world ruled by cynical and shallow people. Life, in my experience, has not been a fairy tale. There is so much cruelty that it's futile to get angry about it. And even as I try to transcend my most superficial materialistic desires, my willpower just crumbles like a stale cookie.

That's why they say you need a strong sense of your self-worth in order to ignore the judgments of others. I understand that in the abstract, but it's putting it into practice that gets me.

Your self-esteem is greatly influenced by how you were raised. It can be weakened by abuse, teasing, neglect, criticism, and a general lack of affection.

But that doesn't mean your self-esteem is fixed. It can change over time. Psychotherapist Nathaniel Branden defined six pillars of self-esteem, which include self-responsibility and self-acceptance. Self-responsibility is a form of confidence that refers to the ability to deal with one's real-life problems, while self-acceptance is about recognizing oneself as worthy of love and respect.

But are we living in a society that allows us to have self-esteem? Even if you were raised in a healthy way, you might come to be rejected from every job you apply to—and even if you do eventually get to work as a cog in a giant corporate machine, you might feel so insignificant that any talk of self-esteem seems a little ridiculous.

Encouraging yourself to accept yourself as you are, in a society that's only too eager to rank us as better or worse, can feel like self-delusion. The world has become a place that is increasingly hostile to self-esteem and the assertion of one's self-worth.

How do we overcome this and stake our place in this cynical world? Two conditions must be met.

First, mutual respect is fundamental. Respect really shouldn't be a scarce resource. It doesn't actually cost anything to respect someone, does it? If respect becomes so common that it's guaranteed for everyone, we won't have to struggle so much to obtain it. Let's make respect a common good. Let's fuel one another with respect. Let's give equal and unquestioned respect to ourselves and others instead of a selective respect that discriminates on the basis of rank and profession and income and appearance.

The second condition is to fundamentally understand and obtain true self-esteem as an individual. To do this, you need to distinguish real self-esteem from fake and fully comprehend the concept. Self-esteem is not the arrogance one feels from superiority or the fleeting satisfaction of being recognized.

The essence of self-esteem is to believe in yourself and to consider yourself worthy of happiness. This isn't the kind of thing that you can just will into being. It's hard to believe in yourself without some kind of action and impossible to do so when you're living contrary to your beliefs. Self-esteem is the inner strength that arises from believing in yourself, being your own person, and living according to your own beliefs, and then taking action and responsibility accordingly.

A Korean television documentary titled *The Private Lives of Children* shows us experiments that demonstrate a parent's effect on a child's self-esteem. Children were given a puzzle to solve, and those whose parents jumped right in to help were determined to have low self-esteem, while those whose parents waited for them to figure it out on their own were determined to have high self-esteem. Belief in and respect for oneself, the major components of self-esteem, are developed by setting one's own goals and solving problems on one's own. Just as the experiment shows us, the most important thing is to have the self at the center.

To be unaware of your own desires and instead let the opinions of others influence you will never help you to develop your self-esteem. The first step to healthy self-esteem is clear: *live as yourself.*

Let's find out what that really means.

✦

Follow, follow me.

To seek self-esteem from
others is to lose control
over your own life.

☑ SEEK OUT YOUR OWN LIFE

Whenever a man in a movie says, "This isn't like you," the woman he's talking to glares at him and replies, "What is 'like me,' then?" She has a point. I get that I need to live my own life, but what does that really mean? And why is it so difficult to figure it out?

The psychologist James Marcia defined four stages of adolescent identity on the path to realizing one's self: diffusion, moratorium, foreclosure, and achievement. Research into Koreans puts most of us (74.4 percent) at a low level, which is foreclosure.

Those in the foreclosure state are subservient to societal norms. This identity state is considered low because those in it lack crises.

No crises in life? That may sound great, but this is not about falling victim to a phishing scheme or being rained on during Monday morning rush hour. It's about a lack of inner struggle over goals, values, and convictions.

Why is there this lack of struggle? It's common in a culture that discourages the exploration or questioning of oneself.

Confucianism, Korea's core philosophy, defines individuals according to their place in society. A person's identity is determined by the role they play, and learning what this role is and how to fulfill it is prioritized over introspection or curiosity. A beautiful life, in other words, is about fitting yourself into societal standards of what a beautiful life is.

And so we're more used to living up to the expectations of our parents than forging our own identities. Many of us don't have the slightest idea of who we are, much less real convictions or a philosophy of life. The deciding factor of why this problem persists is education that refuses to allow freedom of thought.

As children, we're told we're too stupid to think for ourselves and are forced to consider ourselves lesser and inferior. Seeing children in this way, many parents refuse to grant autonomy to their children and deny them the *process* of making themselves into adults. These children, having been denied the *process*, end up with just the *result* of being adults, and they tend to be afraid of making decisions and constantly seek out mentors and parental figures.

But inspirational figures like Pomnyun Sunim and Dr. Oh Eun Young are not going to save you. Learning how to live as yourself is about learning how to judge and decide on your own.

Becoming a freelancer, for example, doesn't necessarily mean you're living as yourself, nor does having a fun hobby. To live as yourself means to understand yourself and make every judgment and decision based on who you are.

It doesn't matter if the wisest of the wise sets up shop next to your home—you must never give up your decision-making to someone else. Your ultimate choices must rely largely on the database that is your past, the wisdom gleaned from your past mistakes, and your inner compass.

^^^^^^^^^^^^^^^^^^^^^^^^^^

ONCE THE CRISIS OF SELF-UNDERSTANDING HAS PASSED, A LIFE IN WHICH YOU BELIEVE IN AND RESPECT YOURSELF CAN FINALLY BEGIN.

^^^^^^^^^^^^^^^^^^^^^^^^^^

If you don't make your own way,
you'll lose yourself.

☑ DON'T DELAY REFLECTING
ON WHAT MAKES YOU HAPPY

There's one comment I always get when I do talks at colleges: "I don't know what I like to do." I always answer with a question: "Was there anything you ever did because you liked doing it?" How many things have you done because you liked doing it, not because you wanted to have done it? We study to go to college, then we work hard to build up our résumés. Is it any wonder that after being educated to suppress our desires all our lives we have no idea what we like to do just for the sake of doing it?

A TV program about children's identity and self-esteem featured a "nice" kid who liked to help others. When the producers asked what he wanted to do, he said, "Help Mom" or "Wash Dad's car." When they asked what he really wanted to do for *himself*, he couldn't answer.

When you occupy yourself in doing things that others expect from you and suppress your own desires, you lose any sense of what you enjoy and what you really want.

Your true happiness will remain an undiscovered land of mystery.

If this isn't what you want, you have to learn to distinguish between what you have to do and what you like to do in order to regain a sense of who you are.

∧∧∧∧∧∧∧∧∧∧∧∧∧∧∧∧∧∧∧∧∧∧∧

NOW IS THE TIME TO ANSWER THE QUESTIONS

YOU'VE DELAYED ANSWERING. WHO ARE YOU,

AND WHAT MAKES YOU TICK?

∧∧∧∧∧∧∧∧∧∧∧∧∧∧∧∧∧∧∧∧∧∧∧

☑ QUESTION WHAT SEEMS OBVIOUS

Once upon a time, a couple, their baby son, and the husband's mother lived in a village where the wife worked the fields. One day, the wife came home to find the senile mother had made chicken soup for lunch. Feeling grateful, she opened the pot only to find not a chicken but her son. Her senile mother-in-law had cooked the baby instead of a chicken. The wife calmed herself down, killed a chicken to serve her mother-in-law, and quietly buried her son. It sounds like something out of a crime drama, but this story became the basis of the filial piety ideal during the Joseon dynasty.

Why is this horrifying infanticide passed down like some chicken-soup-for-the-soul story about a devoted daughter-in-law?

People's emotions were so suppressed back then that even this extreme example of piety was considered a virtue. No matter how infuriating or painful something was, no sacrifice was too big for the sake of "harmony."

Consider how diligence was considered a virtue when I was young. Rain or snow, in sickness or injury, you had to go to school to get that attendance certificate, and the class motto "WORK HARD" was framed above the blackboard. We had such a slogan because Korea was in its industrial hey-day, and manufacturing requires diligence and steadiness more than crea-tivity or individuality.

In such a world, a child can end up cooked in a pot while the mother is celebrated as a model daughter instead of jailed for neglect. A child who goes to school boiling with fever is held up as a model student. The mores of this society turn horror stories into homilies and violence into honor.

We still live as if social norms are universal truths. But what is essential to sustaining our lives are not social norms but our own convictions. So what can we do about this?

A friend who went to the United States to study economics told me that her program had something called Unlearning Class, which is a kind of boot camp in which the brain "unlearns" all the obsolete econ theory students learned as undergrads.

When we learn about the world's famous thinkers, we search for errors in their theories—that's how knowledge advances. We need to question what we've been taught to take for granted and figure out whether our beliefs are what we truly believe or what someone else told us to believe. Only when we question what we've believed all our lives can we take a step for-ward to the future.

^^^^^^^^^^^^^^^^^^^^^^^^^^^
**IN ORDER TO REPLACE SOCIAL NORMS
WITH OUR OWN CONVICTIONS, WE NEED
OUR OWN "UNLEARNING" BOOT CAMP.**
^^^^^^^^^^^^^^^^^^^^^^^^^^^

There's nothing trapping you.

☑ DO NOT LIVE TO PLEASE OTHERS

I don't work a corporate job. Not because I made some grand decision about it or anything, but because there happened to be something I wanted to write, and I decided I'd consider getting a corporate job after I was done. But then . . . I suddenly wondered why I was able to make such an important decision so casually.

I think it was because of the way my parents raised me. I've never had to strive to meet their expectations. They would offer their opinion on any decisions I was making, but in the end they always supported me. And while my older sister was the top student in school—unlike me, who spent all my time reading manhwa comics—they never compared me to her, not even once. I was never afraid of losing their approval, and I got used to making my own decisions.

I still felt some pressure to have them think well of me, of course. But I got rid of it early on when I realized that more pressure did not mean more love. In my midtwenties, in the middle of dinner, I told them, "Set aside your expectations and just think of me as someone who rents from you."

They were upset and said I was being ungrateful after all they'd done to raise me. But I kept repeating that they should think of me merely as their tenant. Sure, I would've loved to be the perfect daughter. We all want our parents to be proud of us, and we try hard to make them proud. But crushing yourself under your own expectations will not make them happy, either, and no matter how much you fret about making them proud, some things just aren't meant to be.

The only thing in our power is to be responsible for ourselves and to hope, but not expect, that the way we live meets our parents' expectations. Living just to satisfy our parents isn't love but a kind of debtor's life. Just as it is up to you to take responsibility for your own life, it is up to your parents to realize their children don't exist to please them.

If what bothers you is your financial debt to your parents, then do your best to repay it. You've got to pay for room and board if you want to be a renter. But don't make your entire life collateral.

THE ONLY EXPECTATIONS YOU NEED

TO STRIVE TO MEET ARE YOUR OWN.

MY WAY OR THE HIGHWAY

☑ DON'T BE ANYONE BUT YOURSELF

In second grade, we were asked what we wanted to be when we grew up. I'd heard about Madame Curie and said I wanted to become a scientist like her. There was no one back then—or now—less likely than I was to become a scientist, but second grade is all about saying whatever you want. It would have been weirder for an eight-year-old to want to work in a trading company or as an accountant in a big chaebol.

The problem is that even as we age, our dreams are often about what we want to *become* rather than what we want to *do*.

I once spoke with a dermatologist who graduated from a medical school in Seoul and worked in the wealthy neighborhood of Gangnam. During our conversation, I felt he had nothing on his mind beyond his work, no personality or philosophy of his own. He gave me the impression that he was a child who hadn't grown up. I asked him if he was happy. Without a second's hesitation, he said, "No." From the outside, he said, it may look like he had a great job, but he really wished he'd gone to a better school and worked at a bigger clinic.

Many people who have high-status jobs are thought to actually be unhappy. He was one of them.

The dermatologist spent his whole childhood studying, and he went to medical school only because he was able to get in. Throughout his studies and residency, he never took the chance to consider other options or think for himself.

Why wasn't he happy? He had pursued status, financial stability, and the approval of others without ever looking inward, which made him feel empty inside. What had mattered to him was becoming a doctor. He had leaned on his professional identity to fill up his empty inner life and compensate for his weak sense of self.

But he was still unhappy. He thought everything would come together once he became a doctor, but he was only obsessed with getting paid more and working at a better place. His emptiness could not be filled just by achieving greater status.

Your job is more than just a means of income, of course. But your job is not synonymous with your self; it doesn't create a self where none is there to begin with.

To pursue superficial goals without reflecting on yourself is to live a life in constant competition with others. It's not a path to true happiness.

WHAT WE DESPERATELY NEED ISN'T A BUSINESS CARD TO PROVE WHO WE ARE BUT TO BECOME A PERSON WHO DOESN'T NEED TO PROVE ANYTHING TO ANYONE.

We do not need to become anyone but ourselves.

☑ DO NOT SIMPLY ACCEPT
THE COMMON VIEW

I once had a conversation with a Canadian who taught English at an elementary school. She was talking about things she found strange in Korea, such as the common belief that a "smart" student meant a "good" student. The way she saw it, a student who wasn't smart could still be good at school, and a smart student could still be bad.

She was skeptical of the equation "smart = good" that Koreans seem to take for granted.

What it means to live well poses a similar problem. There is more to living well than just financial stability: a healthy body, strong relationships, the ability to appreciate art and philosophy, the satisfaction of a job well done. But to Koreans, living well often means just one thing: being rich.

Why have we been programmed to forget all other values and focus on that single one?

This is probably an effect of the 6.25 Mindset and the Red Scare. June 25, the 6.25 in question, is the date in 1950 when the Korean War began, and the 6.25 Mindset is the "live or die" way of thinking that many Koreans adopted after the war—determined never to be invaded again or to experience national despair, the government made us follow national curfews and instilled a militant culture. During the Communist Red Scare, discussion and debate were outlawed in order to enforce conformity and solidarity as a way for us to survive.

The Mindset perpetuated itself for generations. We developed a habit of setting goals that quantified our national objectives in numbers, like "$10 billion in exports, $1,000 in income," which spilled over into personal goals like "Lose ten pounds, get 990 on the TOEIC." It became our cultural habit for all of us to pursue the same objectives. Everyone had to be cheerfully modest, have less than 17 percent body fat while weighing 105 pounds, go to a good school, and work at a chaebol.

There is constant conversation about what the nationwide personal goals should be, accompanied by mass approval of the "right" answer and mass contempt for the "wrong" ones. Whoever is deemed wrong is set out on an ice floe to fend for themselves.

What we're left with is an arrogant minority with the "correct" answer and a helplessly despairing majority with the "wrong" ones.

The British journalist Daniel Tudor described Korea as a pressure cooker, calling it "the impossible country" for imposing on its people unattainable standards of education, prestige, appearance, and professional accomplishment. Is this ideal self even possible? Not everyone can be thin, charming, go to prestigious schools, or work in chaebols. A place where everyone meets these standards would be a fantasy dystopia.

If the world imposes on you a "correct" way of being, you must question it. Don't hold yourself to irrational standards, and don't fault yourself for not conforming to values you don't accept.

^^^^^^^^^^^^^^^^^^^^^^^^^^^

THERE ARE MANY DEFINITIONS OF WHAT A GOOD

STUDENT IS, MANY WAYS OF LIVING A GOOD LIFE,

AND WE EACH HAVE THE RIGHT TO OUR OWN ANSWER.

OUR ANSWERS ARE NOT WRONG, SIMPLY DIFFERENT.

^^^^^^^^^^^^^^^^^^^^^^^^^^^

Those who believe heavy metal to be the ultimate form of music may wish the Beatles had played heavy metal, but whatever music they played, the Beatles would've always been the Beatles.

☑ NURTURE YOUR TASTE

In my twenties, I once read a book on tips and life hacks that the author had accumulated over a lifetime. One tip was about how a few quality garments could bring more satisfaction than many cheap ones.

I recently recalled this little nugget of wisdom when I looked in my closet. There was the winter coat I bought just because it was on sale, the skirt that looked good on a mannequin that I hadn't bothered trying on myself, and highly revealing items that would not pass my mother's veto in the foyer. But I don't regret my past shopping decisions. Through my frequent fashion failures, I've managed to figure out the best style for me and develop my own taste in clothes.

If you've also made many bad choices in clothes, it just means you've made an effort to figure out what works for you. So here's my little life hack: nurture your taste and perspective through failure, or trial and error, to discover your personal style.

^^^^^^^^^^^^^^^^^^^^^^^^^
**LIFE, IN THE END, IS ABOUT PUTTING FORWARD
THE VERSION OF YOURSELF THAT BEST REFLECTS YOU.**

^^^^^^^^^^^^^^^^^^^^^^^^^

✦

The fact that short hair suits *her*, and sports jackets and skinny jeans look good on *him*, and peach-colored foundation makes *my* skin glow, were all discoveries made through brave new experiments.

If I don't do anything, I will never fail at anything!

A life with nothing attempted is like a ship that never sets sail.

Except at life.

☑ HAVE YOUR OWN TASTE

A former boyfriend of mine had a membership to a local arts center and regularly attended their performances, mostly of modern dance and performance art from around the world. He would bring me along because he felt I should be similarly cultured. But aside from that one time they had a flamenco performance, I was bored. I couldn't understand what was going on even after reading the program—I prefer clarity to obscurity. I told him it wasn't to my taste, and he should go with someone else.

I'm not making a judgment on the value of performance art. Some people are moved by modern dance, others by plastic figurines of anime characters, and still others by *Game of Thrones*.

Some make the mistake of assigning a hierarchy to artistic tastes or imposing their tastes on others, but differences in taste are not evidence of superiority or inferiority, nor is your taste something you should force on to others.

To enrich your life, you need to have your own taste. This requires being honest about how you feel. You mustn't be pressured by the judgment of others or seek out activities based on how they might appear on social media. To become deeply aware of your tastes, you do need to make an effort to explore them, but tastes are, in the end, not something to develop but to feel.

I prefer exhibitions to performances, comedies to dramas, and pork rib cold noodle combos to steak with wine.

What we need is not some fancy affectation to put in the "hobbies" section of our résumés but something that our own tastes respond to.

∧∧∧∧∧∧∧∧∧∧∧∧∧∧∧∧∧∧∧∧∧∧∧

TASTE IS WHERE THE SHINE AND DEPTH OF LIFE RESIDE.

∧∧∧∧∧∧∧∧∧∧∧∧∧∧∧∧∧∧∧∧∧∧∧

Respect my taste, goddamn it.

☑ CONFRONT THE REAL YOU

I don't easily forget old slights. "She's selfish." "He's two-faced." "That person's rude." I make these judgments against whoever has wronged me and carry the grudge for a long time, justifying my dislike of them by labeling them "bad people."

But when I've hurt others, on the other hand, I've tended to think, "I just didn't know any better back then" or "That was an honest mistake."

Until one day I began to wonder why I never thought of the wrongs of others in the same way—as the result of being young and not knowing any better, or as honest mistakes. Because everyone has their mean moments and makes mistakes, and weren't they just being immature like I was? In the end, wasn't I the real villain for thinking otherwise?

Up until that point, I had considered only the sides of myself that I liked as "me" and acted like I was perfect. Meanwhile, whenever any side of myself that I didn't like surfaced, I overlooked it—pretending not to see, pretending not to hear. I disguised the parts of me I didn't like as "not-me." How oblivious I was to my own faults.

Carl Gustav Jung, one of the founders of psychoanalysis, called the totality of the things one wants to hide their "shadow." He said we all have a shadow that we cannot eliminate and that we need to make peace with for the sake of our health.

Everyone has flaws they want to hide. But if you hate your inner shadow so much that you refuse to acknowledge it, then your sense of self will get all mixed up inside you, and you'll never know your real self or have control over it.

We need to become more aware and tolerant of our shortcomings as we work toward a healthier inner life. So accept the parts of yourself you don't like too much.

When you see yourself as you really are, you can set the right boundaries and be more generous to those who stay within those boundaries. Only when you stop neglecting and making excuses for yourself and accept the whole you, warts and all—confronting the real you, in other words—can you move past self-righteousness and become a truly human human.

+

We don't hate someone because they aren't perfect. We hate their arrogance when they pretend to be perfect.

None of us is perfect, after all.

☑ DISCOVER WHERE YOU CAN SHINE THE BRIGHTEST

In middle school I volunteered at a local government office with a friend. We had to create lists of documents and compare figures on spreadsheets to see if there were mistakes. I wasn't great with numbers and immediately felt drained at the sight of the documents. As I worked through the tedious pile at a snail's pace, my friend zipped through her share and even said, "That was fun." Fascinated, I asked her what her secret was, and she said catching mistakes gave her a sense of accomplishment. She ended up majoring in accounting and now works at an accounting firm. I'm sure she's an ace at her job and treasured by her employers.

To live a life that honors who you are, you need to understand your talents and find a job where they can shine. Otherwise, your gifts will go to waste and you'll have to endure the agony of feeling that you and what you do are worthless.

When people think about talent, they often think of the arts or specific, measurable, and demonstrable skills, or they consider only extraordinary talent as being worthy of the word. But this mentality can prevent you from recognizing your gifts.

Talent can be developed, and every type can make a contribution. For example, not everyone who excels at writing needs to be a novelist. More important than the level of your talent is to know what specific aptitude you possess and where it will shine.

What is talent, anyway? I think of it as being whatever you can do more easily than others. There are many things that fall into this category. Some people have a talent for working with documents, others find it easy to talk to strangers, others have an eye for detail or beauty, others are excellent listeners. Talents like these are not as obvious as being able to draw or sing. Which is why you have to pay close attention in order to discover your gifts and figure out where you can make the best use of them. Write down what you like and what comes easily to you. If you don't know, take an aptitude test online. There are various ways to find out what you're good at.

Find the common ground between what you want and what you're good at.

^^^^^^^^^^^^^^^^^^^^^^^^^^^^

THERE'S NO SUCH THING AS A TALENTLESS PERSON—

THEY JUST HAVEN'T DISCOVERED THEIR TALENT YET.

^^^^^^^^^^^^^^^^^^^^^^^^^^^^

ME BUYING A TABLET

Draw
Make videos
Create schedules
...

Watch YouTube

Actual use is more important than potential.

☑ NO MATTER HOW GOOD IT SOUNDS, SEE FOR YOURSELF

randomly came across an interview online that was a clip from some documentary.

"At the very least, if you get into a good school in Seoul, you'll make this much money and live in this general region and live out the rest of your life at this level of comfort. Success is happiness, is it not? And in Korea, the first step to happiness is to get into a good university."

They were trying to make it sound like going to a good university guaranteed a good life. There was truth to this idea . . . maybe thirty years ago.

Society is becoming ever more unpredictable, competition is increasing, and going to a good school no longer guarantees a good life. And lots of people become successful regardless of where or whether they went to college. So why do people keep repeating this lie? The interviewee, of course, was the owner of a cram school. Guess who the biggest beneficiary of this type of anxiety would be? A cram school owner. I wonder how many students listened to him and ended up becoming disappointed with life.

The famous marshmallow test is now a classic study in education and psychology. A child is given a marshmallow and told not to eat it for fifteen minutes if they want to be given another one, and the children who manage to wait the fifteen minutes are said to be more likely to become better students later on and be more successful. This experiment is often used to justify sacrificing today's happiness for tomorrow's.

There are other interpretations, however, like how the true variable in this experiment isn't discipline but the stability and trust within the growth environment of the child as well as economic factors that would make the child more disinterested in eating a marshmallow. The classic interpretation, in other words, is hardly the whole story.

The world overflows with formulas for success, with all sorts of stories from people claiming they have found the true path spreading the gospel—for a fee.

Sure, every story has a bit of truth to it. But an individual's success is so dependent on factors like personality, situation, timing, and luck that it's impossible to create a formula for success. This is why you need to cut through all the overpackaging and the padding surrounding these self-help theories to see whether it's all just some greedy, money-grab pyramid scheme. Because if you don't, you'll end up as somebody's tool.

^^^^^^^^^^^^^^^^^^^^^^^^^^^^^^

LEARN INSTEAD OF REVERE,

CREATE INSTEAD OF IMITATE,

GROW INSTEAD OF FOLLOW.

^^^^^^^^^^^^^^^^^^^^^^^^^^^^^^

✦

Become your own light to illuminate the world around you.

Sometimes, what saves us isn't faith but suspicion.

PART THREE

Checklist for Not Being Defeated by Anxiety

Worrying doesn't empty tomorrow of its sorrow—

it empties today of its strength.

—CORRIE TEN BOOM

☑ ENDURE THE UNCERTAINTY THAT IS LIFE

I like to get my fortune told. It's something of a hobby of mine. Lately, I've even started to learn a little about how to read people's fortunes. But how accurate is fortune-telling?

While writing this book, I went to a fortune teller with some friends. I was basically told: "Your book is absolutely going to fail, so if you don't want to starve to death, find an office job."

A very depressing prediction, but seeing as the book didn't fail—quite the opposite, in fact—I wonder if that fortune teller will starve to death before I do.

Some of the fortune tellers I went to were extremely accurate, but seeing how twins born almost at the same time do not live the same lives, even the most famous fortune teller cannot guarantee their predictions 100 percent of the time. Like the Oracle implies in *The Matrix* by not telling Neo whether he is "the one," it's one thing to know the path forward and another thing entirely to walk it.

The thing about fortunes is that they're like red ginseng candy with only 5 percent ginseng—predictions with only a dash of truth—and if we want to know what's really going to happen in life, we have to live it.

Still, we want reassurance, so we go to fortune tellers. But even if Nostradamus were to wake up tomorrow from the dead, we'd still be unsure of the future. Not because fortune tellers are bad at their job, but because life is fundamentally uncertain.

I'm sorry if you're looking for certainties in life, but having spent a pretty penny going to all kinds of fortune tellers for a decade, I can only conclude that life is ultimately about enduring uncertainty.

✦

In the end, we go to fortune tellers to hear them say that things will work out: "Everything will be fine." Instead of believing in them—believe in yourself.

*To want a life of perfect safety, free from
the unexpected or even the inevitable,
is to wish for a life in a bubble. Safety
in life doesn't come from eliminating
uncertainties but from confronting them.*

You're doing fine and you'll be all right.

☑ DON'T ASSUME YOU'RE ALONE
IN YOUR PROBLEMS

From the time we're little, we tend to think a normal household means having parents who get along and give their children unconditional love. Which is why whenever my parents fought, I thought, *Is our family abnormal?* But the older I got, the more I could see how every household has conflicts and problems. The closer they were, the more conflict families often had, and people being as complex as they are, it was natural that they would run into problems living together.

What the media portrays and what people choose to show on social media suggest that picture-perfect families are everywhere. This can lead everyone else to believe that only they are abnormal, and to hide their sense of inferiority deep down inside.

But what does it mean to be abnormal? Does it mean not being picture-perfect? But how could it be normal to not lack a single thing? Could such a life even exist?

Normality is not about being perfect—even Freud acknowledged it was normal to have a drop of hysteria, a smidge of obsession, and a dash of compulsion. Being normal doesn't mean being flawless but having scars, flaws, and shortcomings.

Life takes many forms, and no two lives are the same, and no one's life is perfect. Whatever kind of home you grew up in, and whatever problems or disadvantages you may have had, don't feel shame about it.

Everything is normal.

✦

We hide away so much unhappiness that we've forgotten how all types of unhappiness are universal.

*When something unwelcome happens,
there are those who see it as a misfortune
and others who see it as just part of life.
Your happiness hinges on this distinction.*

☑ DON'T FOLLOW SOME
BS SCRIPT FOR LIFE

There was a time when I kept worrying about unrealistic things. And when the things I worried about didn't actually come to pass, I would be relieved. For example, I exaggerated my worries to comfort myself, to the point that whenever I had a cough I would convince myself it was TB. I was so worried about having tuberculosis that finding out I had the flu was actually good news. My exaggerated worries became habits ingrained in my body, and these dress rehearsals for the worst wore me down.

Worrying about things that haven't happened yet is like living in a bunker because you're scared of the possibility of war or buying a lot of stuff in bulk "just in case."

It is a waste, and completely irrational. How to overcome it? Worry is on the whole irrational and arises from negative thinking. The first step to stop yourself from getting consumed by worry is to rein in your imagination.

Look objectively at your worries. You'll often find that you're imagining the worst-case scenario, which is also the unlikeliest. How likely is it really that a mere cough will turn out to be tuberculosis? Don't ruin the present moment with a catastrophized future.

^^^^^^^^^^^^^^^^^^^^^^^^^^

YOUR ANXIETY COMES FROM YOUR BS SCRIPT FOR LIFE.

^^^^^^^^^^^^^^^^^^^^^^^^^^

We worry about misfortune in the future, but the greatest misfortune is how we ruin our present with worry.

☑ FIND A REAL SOLUTION

There's a primitive thought process we're susceptible to called magical thinking. For example, in ancient times, before we understood how weather really worked, rain that wouldn't stop or typhoons that raged for days were so unexpected and unsettling that they called for extreme interventions. People in those days thought the gods were angry and sacrificed virgins to appease them. But rain stops when it's meant to stop, no matter how many virgins are sacrificed. The belief that fate could be controlled gave people reassurance. Magical thinking refers to what people devise to combat fear and dread in situations where they feel they have no control.

When I was a child, receiving the anti-Communist training that all Korean children were subjected to back then, I prayed before bed each night for a year that there would be no war. While my prayers meant nothing in the context of international political affairs, I believed they could keep war at bay.

Even though we're no longer cavemen or ten-year-olds, we still rely on magical thinking. We may not sacrifice virgins to prevent floods or pray every night to prevent war, but we do continue to invest in solutions that have no effect in the face of whatever feels beyond our control.

Which is why people spend money on shaman rituals to ward off debt or believe a shady boyfriend's feeble excuses—pretending that forgiving him will change him—or obsess over things that have no bearing on their happiness. But the more you rely on false solutions, the more out of reach the real solutions become, and in the end nothing gets resolved. You might believe time will heal your wounds, but just as fairies won't do your homework for you while you're asleep, there are some problems time just can't solve.

If you find yourself unable to get past a problem, ask yourself whether you've been clinging to a false solution instead of confronting the true nature of your problem. Although it may take a while, ultimately you have to turn your worry into an action plan. But only that first step toward a real solution will eventually free you from the problem.

✦

Liberation means recovering your inner consciousness. Free yourself from what has held you back for so long.

*When looking back at the past, what
you need is analysis, not regret.*

And when looking ahead to the future,
what you need is judgment, not worry.

☑ TRY NOT TO BE OVERSENSITIVE

My friend was in a car accident once. She was crossing the street when a stopped car lurched forward and hit her. Luckily, she wasn't badly hurt. But ever since hearing the story, I'm watchful of even stopped cars whenever I cross the street.

Anxiety is the vague sense that bad experiences may happen again. When you've lived a certain number of years, you'd think the variety of your experiences would give you a broader perspective, but the traumas you've accumulated actually give you more fodder for anxiety. And just like with my experience of my friend's accident, anxiety can be passed on second-hand.

We live in a world with too many things to be anxious about. The media reports all sorts of accidents every day, even every few minutes. We're besieged by news of medical emergencies and economic instability. People are on edge, and our online communities are replete with reports of the worst kinds of real-life tragedies.

Having been subjected to all this news, we can't help being anxious. We cycle through endless feedback loops of anxiety. Our sensitized minds break down the barriers between reality and our fears, making us fragile in the face of the smallest setbacks.

To cope, you have to try to bring your hypersensitive mind down a notch. Tell yourself that the past is in the past, there's no proof that things will become worse, and you can't live in constant fear of every possible disaster.

Relax your mind and let it return to the real world, not the world of your imagination.

^^^^^^^^^^^^^^^^^^^^^^^^^^^^

THE LIFE YOU ARE *ACTUALLY* EXPERIENCING IS A LOT MORE PEACEFUL THAN YOU THINK, AND YOU ARE STRONGER THAN YOU REALIZE.

^^^^^^^^^^^^^^^^^^^^^^^^^^^^

Spices that enhance flavor can ruin a dish when applied in excess.

☑ BE JUST THE NECESSARY AMOUNT OF SAD

We say goodbye to a lot of things in life: a loved one; our childhood, when we may not have received the love we needed; ideals that we once held so close; our youth; a time in which we believed in ourselves. All such partings need to be mourned, for long or short periods.

To mourn means to be sad without restraint. But often we find ourselves too scared to confront loss, and instead we suppress or ignore or misunderstand our need to mourn, refusing to give ourselves the chance to be sad.

Freud says that when we do not mourn properly, we become depressed. Emotions do not simply disappear when we plug them up and prevent them from leaking out. Without the mourning process to wash away our sadness, our emotions stagnate into a pool of depression and prevent us from moving on with our lives.

If you find yourself experiencing anxiety or depression, find the source of it. Even if it may be hidden or distorted, keep questioning yourself and seeking clues to confront it. Knowing what your emotions really stem from may be the end of the search but not the anxiety or depression itself. Simply understanding where it comes from may not be enough to throttle it, and you may need time to adequately mourn.

Ask the deepest part of yourself: What have you parted with?

∧∧∧∧∧∧∧∧∧∧∧∧∧∧∧∧∧∧∧∧∧∧∧∧∧∧

FOR ALL THE INEVITABLE GOODBYES,

WE MUST TAKE THE TIME TO MOURN.

∧∧∧∧∧∧∧∧∧∧∧∧∧∧∧∧∧∧∧∧∧∧∧∧∧∧

Thinking deeply about what's important   Thinking superficially about many things

To discover the true nature of a problem,
we need not more thought but more depth of thought.

☑ WHEN THINGS ARE HARD, SAY THEY'RE HARD

'm not the type to go around saying I'm having a hard time. Not only do I hate telling people I'm suffering but I also tend not to think of myself as someone who suffers. It feels like talking about it would make it worse, so I always end up saying, "I'm OK."

But suppressing my feelings only makes me less sensitive to myself. This in turn makes me insensitive to other things, and I begin to neglect my feelings as I keep working through the pain, unaware that I am nearing my limit.

Which is why we need to speak up when things are hard, even when no one listens or there's no change in the situation. We also need to rest for a bit when things get to be too much. You can't always rein in your feelings by saying that you're fine, and you can't always be strong.

So when you feel like you're drowning in responsibilities, or when you want to cry the second you get home from work, just say, "I'm having a hard time."

No one but you can take care of yourself, and at some point self-sacrifice becomes simply self-abuse. It's all right to be a little selfish, a little irresponsible. But nothing is more irresponsible than neglecting yourself while claiming to be responsible.

+

In that spirit: lately I've been having a really hard time.

I guess I'm having a hard time.

Ignoring feelings doesn't make them better—acknowledging them does.

☑ TAKE TIME TO PROCESS THINGS

The Grant Study at Harvard University tracks a person's whole life, partly to determine what the conditions of true happiness are. According to one of the study's lead researchers, George Vaillant, the deciding factor for a person's success and happiness in life lies in their subconscious defense mechanisms, specifically in how they respond to adversity. Vaillant identifies four levels of defense mechanisms—pathological, immature, neurotic, and mature—and argues that most psychological problems stem from issues that arise in our various developmental stages.

But there was a particular example that surprised me. It was about a woman who desperately wanted a child, but she was diagnosed with uterine cancer and had to get a hysterectomy. After waking up from the procedure, instead of feeling profound sadness she spoke of being more sympathetic to the suffering of those around her. Of how she had actually experienced an awesome form of luck and that it had been a blessing to discover her cancer at an early stage and undergo a successful operation.

So—would this be an example of a mature or immature defense mechanism? Apparently it's the latter. But why would such acceptance and even transcendence be considered immature?

While her reaction may resemble the mature defense mechanism of "sublimation," it's actually a form of "disassociation" in which an unbearable situation causes one to separate oneself from the source of trauma. In other words, it's an immature response masking itself as a mature one. How, then, are we to tell the difference between a mature and an immature defense mechanism?

The difference is in whether the response stems from a proper reckoning: experiencing one's sadness, undertaking a thoughtful processing of what happened, and facing up to reality for what it is.

^^^^^^^^^^^^^^^^^^^^^^^^^^^

TO IMITATE MATURITY WITHOUT PROPERLY PROCESSING WHAT HAS HAPPENED IS JUST SELF-DECEPTION AND NOT A TRUE SOLUTION.

^^^^^^^^^^^^^^^^^^^^^^^^^^^

We hear the same things all the time: to respect yourself, to accept yourself as you truly are, and to love yourself.

All good points. We absolutely should treat ourselves this way.

But we can't love ourselves by just pretending to do so or simply by repeating the words over and over again. Loving and respecting yourself come about only through a process of internal growth, which is possible only through persistent resistance of self-hate, the willingness to stop dwelling in hurtful memories, and facing yourself as you are. Only through nurturing your internal strength can self-love truly be achieved.

Of course, this is easier said than done. But only those who have walked the long and hard path can bring true self-love to fruition.

Let's stop all this pretending to love ourselves. Let's try to really love ourselves.

I certainly hope I do, and I hope you do as well.

☑ DON'T DO SOMETHING
JUST BECAUSE YOU'RE ANXIOUS

I worked really hard from college up until now. I won a major contest, paid to participate in some weird leadership program, and supported many causes. But I also did a lot of things that don't really help me now.

Of course, all experience is useful to some degree—like how Steve Jobs learning calligraphy led to Apple's typography designs. But we do not have infinite amounts of time, and only when we have a focal point for our efforts can all of our peripheral experiences also have meaning. And yet, because we live in a world where we feel constant pressure to be productive and to improve, we're always doing *something*, and doing so reassures us.

But how can I justify a beginner's level coding class when all I can do is print "Hello world" or a bogus certificate for some quirky hobby or all the other pursuits I have no memory of? They don't guarantee any benefits in life, and whatever sense of accomplishment they provide is quick to evaporate.

The world is full of schemes to profit off our anxiety, and without a sense of what's important, we fall for them. So quit being chased around by your worries, your desperate attempts not to fall behind the pack, your elaborate efforts to prove you're working hard. Instead, go back to basics.

^^^^^^^^^^^^^^^^^^^^^^^^^^^^

WHAT KIND OF A PERSON ARE YOU? WHAT ARE

THE THINGS YOU CAN DO FOR YOUR OWN SAKE?

^^^^^^^^^^^^^^^^^^^^^^^^^^^^

Set a goal and start on the path toward it. Being conscious of your goal and achieving it—that's where true relief lies.

Running without thinking means you'll never reach your destination.

☑ LEARN TO GO ON WITH YOUR DAY
EVEN WHEN THERE'S A PROBLEM

Unexpected problems will always pop up in life. Many of them have no immediate solution. Things you can't take back. Past mistakes that haunt you in the present. Tasks you constantly need to take care of so they don't snowball. Obstacles that make you want to throw away your whole life and start over.

If only we could reset our lives like in a video game. But just because something went wrong, should we live our life like we're dead until the next one?

I've certainly had moments of despair. But whenever I've had them, I would always conclude that I wanted to keep on living. It just wasn't fair that I should give up my whole life for one mistake, and while my life may seem insignificant to others, it's the only one I have. Like what the title character says in *Another Miss Oh*, I still loved myself and wished myself a hopeful future.

You might be in that situation now. Exhausted, sick of yourself, life getting you down—you might want to throw in the towel. But you are the only real caretaker of your life. Just because you got hurt or you're dissatisfied, you can't leave your life all alone in the dark to cry. That's irresponsible. If something bad happens, being sad about it for a while and letting yourself process the pain will eventually lead you to find a way to live with it.

Not for silly reasons like your pain isn't significant or because "everyone else deals with it"—but because your life is precious to you, I sincerely hope that you live it well.

*The best we can do is to live as true
to the moment as possible.*

PART FOUR

Checklist for Living with One Another

When people ganged up on me, I just thought, "By cursing me out, you bastards don't hurt me, and if you were to praise me, that wouldn't make me any better than I already am. So do whatever you want to do, since I can't be beaten down or lifted up by you, and I'll just keep living my life the way I want."

–KIM HOON IN THE INTERVIEW "KIM HOON IS KIM HOON AND PSY IS PSY" BY KIM GYEONG

☑ HAVE AT LEAST A BASIC LEVEL OF RESPECT FOR ONE ANOTHER

A story about a man who went missing and was found dead once went viral. Netizens were speculating wildly about whether the man had been murdered, died of suicide, or was the victim of an accident. But whatever the manner of his death, isn't the fact that he is no longer alive tragedy enough? To anyone just reading about it, a tragic story can become fodder for gossip. To an outsider, a slum could seem romantic, or to a traveler, an "experience."

Granted, it's human nature to be curious about the hardships that befall others. But what if others did that to you—would you allow it? No one should have the right to violate the privacy of others.

If you do not want to find yourself being gossiped about by strangers, you need to protect the privacy of others as well. You can't create an exclusive zone of protection for yourself and not make an effort to safeguard the lives of others. You can't demand the right to be forgotten when you demand the right to know the business of others.

Curb your curiosity about other people's business. That's the best way to protect your own privacy and is the least we can do to respect one another.

☑ DON'T TRY SO HARD TO BE UNDERSTOOD BY EVERYONE

*A*re you getting married? Do you have a job? A boyfriend? What about your savings? People think these questions are rude. But it's not the questions themselves that are rude; it's the judgment behind them.

It's the scrutiny of those who think anyone outside their idea of the norm is "wrong"—they're like psychologists or criminal profilers who think they're neutral and unbiased, when they don't even know the first thing about themselves.

But just as a math student who can't solve a quadratic equation is the one at fault and not the quadratic equation itself, someone's inability to understand us is not our fault but that of the other person.

There's no need to care about such people or to strive to prove yourself to them.

∧∧∧∧∧∧∧∧∧∧∧∧∧∧∧∧∧∧∧∧∧∧∧∧

WE'RE NOT HERE TO GET VALIDATION

FROM THE PREJUDICED. YOUR LIFE,

IN THE END, IS YOUR OWN.

∧∧∧∧∧∧∧∧∧∧∧∧∧∧∧∧∧∧∧∧∧∧∧∧

✛

Those who conflate all third-person perspectives into the omniscient are bound to always misread the situation.

*But I'm not here
to be understood by you.*

✓ RESPECT ONE ANOTHER'S BOUNDARIES

have a friend who's always cheerful. I've never seen her depressed or stressed over projects in college or late nights at the office. Everyone is fascinated by her attitude. Is such a carefree person truly possible?

As her friend for over a decade, I can assure you that she's not all sunshine and lollipops—she's as complex as anyone else. It's true that she has good physical and mental health and isn't oversensitive. But she also keeps personal boundaries that she never oversteps or allows anyone else to overstep. This isn't because she's full of dark secrets; it's just that everyone has their own personal space and a different sense of where they feel their boundaries should be.

Ever since we were little, we've gotten used to others violating our boundaries in the name of friendship or family—a violation often dressed up as intimacy.

But opening yourself up fully and losing your boundaries are not prerequisites of a good relationship, and we can't demand that someone lower their guard in the name of friendship. Even if you think someone has too many boundaries, it is not your business to go hacking away at them from the outside. Violating someone's personal boundaries is a form of violence. A good relationship requires that we respect each other's boundaries, and a good friendship includes the ability to enjoy each other's company from a comfortable distance.

✚

Even though she doesn't share everything with me, I consider her a great friend.

Don't mistake a violation of boundaries for intimacy.

☑ BECOME A GENEROUS INDIVIDUALIST

The book *The Courage to Be Disliked* became a bestseller in both Korea and Japan. It sold so well it became worthy of the label "phenomenon." Why did it do so well in these two countries? Interestingly, both Korea and Japan are often said to have low levels of happiness despite their wealth.

Why is that? A country's level of individualism is an important cultural factor related to happiness, and its happiness-inducing effects are decoupled from wealth. Rich countries with low levels of individualism tend to be less happy. This describes super-collectivist countries like Korea and Japan.

What is it about collectivism that inhibits happiness? Collectivism prizes harmony, emphasizing the good of the group over the good of the individual and exerting control over individuals for the sake of community, which is exhausting enough. But the bigger problem is how this control becomes internalized within individuals.

If an individualistic society uses someone's guilt, or private shame, to control and regulate their citizens, collectivist societies use humiliation, or public shame. Humiliation is shame seen through the eyes of others, which leads to a constant awareness of others, letting their gaze affect our every movement. We put ourselves in other people's shoes and say things like, "I'll show them, I'll show all of them" and "No one will be able to look down on me anymore."

It's like having a surveillance camera on your soul. The thought that someone is watching keeps you tense and anxious. The fact that a book like *The Courage to Be Disliked* was a publishing phenomenon in Korea and Japan is proof of our fatigue of collectivism, where we live in constant fear of others' judgment.

The reason we became a collectivist society is that we come from agrarian origins where collective labor was crucial. But it's not like everyone is growing rice nowadays. What we need more than the courage to be disliked is a tolerant individualism. I'm not saying everything foreign is good. It's just that we need to balance out some of the collectivism in our society. We should keep a bird's-eye view on society but still allow for individuality and personal freedom.

Not to mention the fact that research shows individualism doesn't increase antisocial behavior like one would expect but correlates with politeness, generosity, and social responsibility. It's because individuals are respected for who they are that more meaningful relationships can be built.

I think two things would improve society: One, to not be nosy about other people; this is a matter of personal responsibility. Two, to not be preoccupied with what other people think; we should accept one another's values and lifestyles and learn to coexist. I'm not perfect in either regard, but I'm trying.

FOR THE SAKE OF YOUR HAPPINESS AS WELL AS OTHERS',

BE MORE GENEROUS TOWARD OTHERS AND YOURSELF.

A little less worrying, a little more respect.

☑ STOP MAKING LIFE ABOUT WINNING OR LOSING

During college orientation, I had the following conversation with a girl in my year. She graduated from an arts high school in Seoul that had sent a few other kids to our department. Fascinated, I said, "It must be nice to be here with friends from high school."

"They're not my friends," she said.

"What? Why not?"

"They're just competitors."

What was this, a high school drama?

I was ultimately the one who was naïve. We were all already deeply competitive. Even I had read books about how to improve your academic standing, one of which said to visualize your nemesis while studying. I designated a classmate of mine as my nemesis, but it didn't last long. The country was filled with kids who were better at school than I was, and it seemed silly to try to beat just one kid. But how many other kids had taken the same advice and made nemeses?

Childhood should be a period of forging lifelong friendships, but instead we are encouraged to compete against our friends for grades and to get into the best colleges. Our peers are regarded as competitors, not as trusted neighbors. Which is why, despite being a very collectivist society, Korea ranks low in community and social relationships in the Organization for Economic Cooperation and Development (OECD).

Ironically, we're actually less community-minded than the individualistic West. This means we act with an awareness of the gaze of others, as per strongly collectivist social mores, but there is no trust or solidarity in that gaze. Our relationships suffocate us and make us feel lonely at the same time. And that exhausts us.

What do we even gain from all of this? Does our competitiveness give us an edge? I don't think so. Bong Joon-ho won the Academy Award for Best Picture by pushing the quality of his moviemaking to his limits, not because he was determined to outdo Martin Scorsese or Quentin Tarantino.

If you find yourself constantly tallying your wins and losses or unwilling to give even an inch to someone else or feeling jealous of a friend's good fortune, you may simply be too accustomed to a competitive society. But competition only makes us exhausted and tense. Competition does not guarantee a competitive edge. Instead of torturing yourself by making everyone your nemesis, find your real purpose and build a world of your own.

And beyond that, recover your trust in others and find a community where you aren't constantly ranking one another.

∧∧∧∧∧∧∧∧∧∧∧∧∧∧∧∧∧∧∧∧∧∧∧∧

ONLY BY BUILDING YOUR OWN SPACE

WITHIN THE SAFETY OF A COMMUNITY CAN

YOUR STRENGTHS AND POTENTIAL TRULY SHINE.

∧∧∧∧∧∧∧∧∧∧∧∧∧∧∧∧∧∧∧∧∧∧∧∧

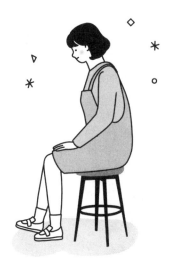

No one ever stole your happiness from you.

☑ DON'T BE A NICE PERSON
JUST TO AVOID BEING DISLIKED

When I was little, I loathed two-faced people so much that I would publicly call them out and humiliate them (I'm not saying I'm proud of this). Thanks to that, I had many enemies.

But it's actually not that pleasant to think of people hating you, even if there's no chance you'll ever see them in person. And I did want to become a nicer person. I thought that even if I heard someone was saying bad things about me, everything would be fine as long as I didn't react. But despite my efforts, I was never going to be what others consider a "nice" person, and instead I ended up becoming someone who couldn't stand up for herself.

Why did I feel I had to be a nice person? I still do, to an extent. I want to be nice to myself, to the people who are close to me, to those who need my help.

But trying to be nice to everyone, even to strangers who judge you without knowing you, is like forfeiting the right to self-defense. I have to have self-respect, and someone's dislike for me doesn't really affect my life in any way. Which is why I stopped making an effort to be nice just for the sake of not being disliked.

It is important not to hurt others, but it is everyone's right and responsibility to stand up for themselves.

+

Note to my enemies: I will destroy you.

Do you think I'm off-the-wall? You're right. Be careful.

Preemptive strikes are illegal,
but self-defense isn't.

☑ DO NOT BE ASHAMED OF THINGS YOU HAVE NO REASON TO BE ASHAMED OF

When my mother was little, she suffered a fever that left her with facial nerve palsy, which I never found strange. I went on a class picnic with her in third grade, and a girl in my class said my mother's face was weird. Bear in mind that when I was a child I was so shy that even in my kindergarten swim class, I would change in and out of my clothes away from everyone else. But hearing my classmate say my mother's face was weird didn't make me feel ashamed. Mother simply had the aftereffects of a fever on her face—why should anyone be ashamed of that?

A friend's friend stayed at a postnatal spa, and one of the women asked everyone what their husbands' jobs were, what kind of house they lived in, and whether they owned or rented. This busybody proceeded to exchange numbers with only a few people, depending on their answers. How rude and crass, to judge strangers in this way. My friend who heard this story from her friend ended up keeping her distance from the other women during *her* postnatal spa stay. And so the vicious cycle continues. The crass ones are the problem, but their victims are the ones who end up feeling hurt and threatened and who withdraw socially.

But why should *we* be embarrassed? Who should actually be embarrassed?

Just because some people are shameless doesn't mean you should feel ashamed of yourself in their place. Even if you can't quite tell them to shut the hell up, **let's not be ashamed about things that we have no reason to be ashamed of.**

+

Those who are quick to laugh at others are the most laughable of all.

What's it to you?

On a TV show, when a female singer pointed at another singer's breasts and asked, "What, are those fake?" the other singer said, "Fake or not, what's it to you?"

Exactly. What's it to you?

☑ YOU DON'T NEED TO GET ALONG WITH EVERYONE

A neighborhood grandmother visited my friend and asked if she could come over from time to time. My friend, who found it hard to say no to things, said yes. Then the grandmother's granddaughter visited and tried to get my friend into her weird religion, then came back for further visits with her cult members.

There are people everywhere who take advantage of the politeness of others. Sometimes you need to hit the brakes on having manners. Even if it makes you feel awkward, you need to express your needs, say no to things, and insist on your boundaries. No doubt this is easier said than done, and I struggle with it myself. But what would I be giving up to be considered a "nice person"? Would the discomfort I'd get in return be worth it?

If being a nice person means having to deal with an intolerable level of discomfort and abuse, it's better to be picky. Protecting your peace doesn't mean you're not nice. Besides, if someone is good enough to keep as a friend, they should respect your boundaries. If they are easily offended when you set limits, they're not someone you need to hold on to.

We shouldn't feel entitled to encroach on the boundaries of others, and we should definitely not let others feel entitled to encroach on ours.

∧∧∧∧∧∧∧∧∧∧∧∧∧∧∧∧∧∧∧∧∧∧∧∧∧

THERE IS NO WAY YOU CAN GET ALONG WITH EVERYONE.

I'M SORRY TO SAY THIS, BUT THE PERSON YOU NEED

TO TAKE CARE OF FIRST IS ALWAYS YOURSELF.

∧∧∧∧∧∧∧∧∧∧∧∧∧∧∧∧∧∧∧∧∧∧∧∧

Those who really care about us would never ask us for too much.

☑ LEARN TO DISTINGUISH BETWEEN SOMETHING BEING WORN AND BEING RUINED

When I get a new phone, my heart sinks if I get a scratch on it, even a small one. Since scratches are inevitable, it's better to accept them rather than let them upset you. If every time something got a scratch we acted as if it were ruined, we'd go bankrupt from having to buy new things all the time.

This type of wear-and-tear mindset applies to relationships, too. Even the best ones sustain some damage, and it's impossible to never be disappointed in someone. If the damage is great, of course, it's better to part ways. But if you keep rejecting people because of inevitable life frictions, you'll be left all alone.

Being a perfectionist about relationships leads only to loss.

Take care to distinguish between ordinary wear and tear in a relationship and something it can't survive. Depending on the strength of the relationship, the scratches may be easily buffed away.

Don't throw away a good friend because you expect only a best friend.

☑ DO YOUR BEST FOR YOUR CURRENT RELATIONSHIPS

As I went from my teens to my twenties and then into my thirties, my list of friends went through a few edits. There are friends who have never fallen from their high spots, those who've grown so distant I wouldn't even know how to contact them, and new friends whom I share everything with. Thinking about the friendships that have fallen away or the ones that felt like they would stand the test of time, I feel guilty about my failures. Why was I so immature? Would I act differently today?

But just as I had my limits, my friends had their limits, too—and since we can't hold on to every relationship we've ever had, the weaker ones inevitably wear out or fall away. This doesn't mean we're bad people; the end of a friendship is simply a fact of life sometimes. There's no need to blame yourself for failed relationships or to worry about losing the ones you have now. Just be the best person you can be to those around you and be open to making friends with new people you meet.

^^^^^^^^^^^^^^^^^^^^^^^^

JUST AS YOU NEED SOMEONE, SOMEONE ALSO NEEDS YOU.

THIS IS HOW EVERYONE SURVIVES IN THIS WORLD

DESPITE THEIR IMPERFECTIONS.

^^^^^^^^^^^^^^^^^^^^^^^^

Not the cherry blossoms of spring
or the rainbow after a storm
or the comets in the sky
can last forever
so just enjoy them in the moment.

☑ GO FULL STEAM AHEAD
WHEN THERE'S A GREEN LIGHT

When you have a crush on someone, it's understandable that you'll read into how they respond to you, looking for a green light, a sign to proceed. But even the lack of a response could have many explanations:

1. Their fingers broke.
2. You're out of sight, out of mind.
3. They're busy with work.
4. They're waiting for you to call first.

And there may well be other reasons for their silence. It's never just one thing; every situation is different. Not even a relationship master or legendary tarot reader can fully understand the intentions of someone else.

And if you still want to know if you have a green light, then the most appropriate question wouldn't be "What does this person think of me?" but "What do I think of this person?"

If the answer is "I like this person," then *that* is your green light to approach them.

+

Don't love because it happens. Make love happen.

☑ EXPRESS YOUR FEELINGS

I recently came across a meme about relationships that said a partner who never gets angry but is always accommodating is a considerate person who has given their all to a relationship and can leave that relationship with no regrets. Therefore, it concluded, one must always do their best to be accommodating.

I found this a little odd. Was that really being considerate? Who wants to be with someone who is smiling on the outside but counting the number of strikes on the inside before finding an out?

The crux of my issue with this meme is the suppression of one's dissatisfaction. Those who avoid expressing themselves take solace in the fact that they can decide to leave whenever they want—their only expression of discontent is their leaving.

This lack of self-expression may look like devotion, but it's more a kind of passive-aggressiveness—a way to cast oneself as a victim enacting revenge against the unjust.

Are such attacks against the unjust justified? Who deserves to throw the first stone? Everyone has been inadvertently unkind to someone. We tend to remember the injustices perpetuated against us more than those we've perpetuated against others, and we all have different ideas of what is right and wrong.

That's why it's important to express our feelings to one another. Just like our cars beep at us in warning when we're parallel parking, we need to express our consternation when other people get too close to the limits of our tolerance. The power to sever a personal connection at any time is not a form of self-esteem, and as long as one runs away from the need to express oneself, relationships will always prove troublesome.

^^^^^^^^^^^^^^^^^^^^^^^^^^^

LEARN HOW TO EXPRESS YOURSELF,

NURTURE HEALTHY RELATIONSHIPS,

AND BUILD YOUR LIFE WITHIN

THOSE RELATIONSHIPS.

^^^^^^^^^^^^^^^^^^^^^^^^^^^

Expressing yourself is difficult, and it's not the advice you might've wanted to hear, but it's what we need to learn for the sake of finding true happiness.

*Being considerate is about the way
you express something,
not about whether you express it.*

☑ FIND SOMEONE TO BE WITH

There has been a spate of bestsellers about how to be happy when alone. Can they be right? Can people truly be happy living alone?

In a book called *The Origin of Happiness* by Dr. Eunkook M. Suh, our DNA is described as our ancestors' survival guide. Our stress systems are activated when we do things that are not conducive to survival, and our dopamine surges when we do things that are. Which means that not eating well makes us stressed and eating well makes us happy. It's all in our DNA.

What were the most important things our ancestors needed for survival?

Surely it was food and people. Let's go back to the days of the archaeopteryx. For our ancestors, deviation from the herd meant instant death. So when a relationship goes bad, the stress is so great because the end of the relationship represents a threat to our very survival. Loneliness equals death.

We no longer need to feel stressed about where to find food—it's all around us—and yet food remains a significant source of stress. To those exhausted by the threat signals from both food and relationships, the bestselling book about loneliness and our DNA would seem like sweet relief.

The book isn't wrong. Unless the world turns into something like *The Walking Dead*, it doesn't matter if someone hates you or likes you. When you're hungry, you have your credit card. When you're in danger, you can call the police. When you're worried about the future, call your insurance company. It's a new world. Being a loner isn't such a big deal anymore. (Yay!) Aside from some oversensitive DNA feedback, it's fine to be disliked. The one problem in all this good news is that our DNA has not kept pace with this new world. Because relationships were the most important factor in our survival, our greatest happiness comes from forming strong ones, just as our biggest stress comes from interpersonal conflict.

It might sound old-fashioned, but like it or not, we are happiest when we're with someone. This is not a matter of literature but of evolutionary psychology, not of sentiment but of instinct.

So don't choose the hard path because you've been burned before. Find someone who is on your wavelength. No need to give up food because of one bout with food poisoning or to cloister yourself just because you met one bad person. The important thing is to avoid spoiled food and to try to keep away from bad people.

Find a friend who can understand and respect you no matter your situation, someone who won't mock you for your shortcomings. And once you do, be that person for them in return. That's the best kind of antianxiety pill and the most reliable path to happiness.

+

What you need from your friend who's late isn't an excuse but an apology. What you need in order to talk to your crush isn't a magic sign but courage. And what you need when you're lonely isn't the power to withstand loneliness but a true companion.

*Hey, friend, when life was hard and the
unexpected hit, what helped me through
those moments that I could not explain—
or didn't want to—were not any grand
gestures but your calm empathy.*

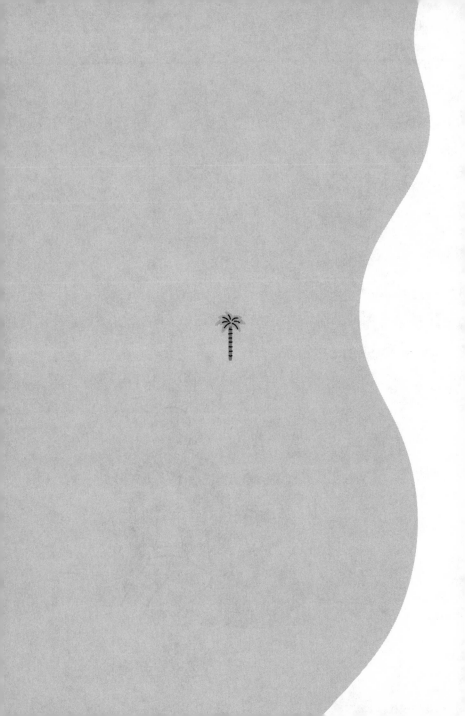

PART FIVE

Checklist for a Better World

Every country has the government it deserves.

—JOSEPH DE MAISTRE

☑ DON'T PUT YOURSELF DOWN

On some TV talk show, a young man in the audience said to his mother, on camera, "Mom, someday I'll buy you a Benz," and the mother looked on with a satisfied smile. Sure, it's a nice sentiment. But maybe I'm a little perverse for finding it sad. I'm sorry to say this, but the odds of this kid buying his mother a Mercedes-Benz are minuscule. Not because of any shortcomings on his part, but because the economic odds are stacked against him.

They say that the moment the umbilical cord appears, the child sucks money out of the parent. Education is expensive, with schools being so competitive. College tuition keeps rising, and the cost of room and board adds thousands a month.

Sure, some households do better than others, but most children are in astronomical debt to their parents by the time they leave the house. Which is why they say things like they'll buy their parents a Benz. Because having broken their parents' backs, it's like they see a Benz as the only thing that could adequately compensate.

The problem lies in how challenging it is to repay this debt. Unemployment is high. People enter the workforce later and later in life. Only 5 percent of those who apply get chaebol jobs (even then, Benzes are out of the question), and as for the rest, they'll be employed but struggling financially. It would be impossible for a couple to get married and be able to afford rent without a loan from a bank or their parents.

Once the couple has kids, the cycle begins all over again, and never in that cycle comes a day when you can afford to buy your parents that Benz.

What makes this situation worse is how it's become taboo to say anything that might trod on the dreams and potential of our children, that despite the need to look reality in the face to find workable solutions, all we let ourselves talk about is a fantasy of success for a minority of children. In the end, too many children grow up to feel loss and despair because they entered the world with dreams, but all they can afford are dregs.

And nowhere did they do anything wrong.

The real culprits are the high cost of living and education, and the lack of jobs that pay well enough to allow people to afford them—all things that are largely out of our hands. We live in a society that forces us into debt even before we grow up, one that doesn't present a way to pay off that debt and makes us suffer the guilt over our own imagined deficiencies.

If you also suffer from feelings of guilt and inadequacy, you should at least understand how you became a debtor. While this knowledge won't pay your debts for you, it'll at least help you not to blame yourself. A society that creates debtors out of ordinary people is a sick society.

^^^^^^^^^^^^^^^^^^^^^^^^^^^^^^

YOUR DEBT IS NOT A RESULT OF LIVING YOUR LIFE WRONG.

^^^^^^^^^^^^^^^^^^^^^^^^^^^^^^

I'm sorry for being ordinary.

(You've done nothing wrong.)

☑ **WHEN YOU NEED TO, BEAR IT**

A coworker from my first job whom I'm still friends with is diligent and polite. But she can't stand it when her employers treat her like she's expendable.

Her boss once made a huge show of giving her a tiny bonus, and when she didn't act sufficiently grateful, he said, "Should I take it back?" My friend was so angry that she threw the money back at him along with her letter of resignation. The company begged her to stay.

He was quite a piece of work, from what I've heard. Who would joke about pay like that? Still, I told my friend not to quit. And who am I to say that to her?

One of my bosses once exaggerated the number of people who had applied for a new position and said to me, "Lots of other designers out there, watch your back," implying that I was replaceable. So I said, "You know what, why don't I quit? Then you get to pick *two* people." Sure, I was younger then, and did so much work that they couldn't possibly fire me, but my friend was in the same kind of situation. Still, I told her not to be so quick to want to quit, that she should quit only when she absolutely had to. Even if this boss was so horrible that he joked about her pay and expected her to act grateful for the bone he threw her once in a while, she shouldn't have to upend her life because of him. To quit because of him is to give him that much more power. Surely he isn't worth that much in her life?

There's no reason to forgive them or smile for them, and you'll need to find a way to deal with their rudeness; still, if you need to be where you are now, bear it.

^^^^^^^^^^^^^^^^^^^^^^^^^^^^

YOU MAKE YOUR OWN DECISIONS, AND IT'S HARDLY SHAMEFUL TO ENDURE A DIFFICULT JOB. IT'S A MATTER OF PRIORITIZING YOUR OWN LIFE OVER BAD PEOPLE.

^^^^^^^^^^^^^^^^^^^^^^^^^^^^

☑ REAL CHANGE TAKES TIME

The sociologist Nho Myung-woo of Ajou University says that although the world feels like it's changing fast, it's actually changing *very slowly*. Kind of like a clinically obese person who after three months of extreme exercising brings their weight down to healthy levels but has trouble maintaining it without great effort because their metabolism hasn't adjusted yet.

Our bodies, personal problems, and social issues do not change immediately, and changes are never permanent. Just as maintenance and vigilance are key to preventing the yo-yo effect, you need time and continuous effort to effect real change, even if it means you have to backtrack or you feel like you're running in place. That's just the way it is.

^^^^^^^^^^^^^^^^^^^^^^^^^^^

THE MOST IMPORTANT WAY TO MAKE

MEANINGFUL CHANGE IS TO BE PATIENT.

^^^^^^^^^^^^^^^^^^^^^^^^^^^

HOW TO PREVENT SCARRING FROM A BURN

1. Apply ointment.   2. Apply it often.   3. Keep applying.

There's no other way.

*The best way to treat a wound
is to try to heal a little bit every day.*

☑ SOMETIMES, SHIFT TO NEUTRAL

I was always a lurker on the internet, but there was a time when I wished I was part of a community of like-minded people. My political convictions were stronger back then, so I joined a political community. I agreed with about 90 percent of the opinions expressed there, which was a fun experience. The problem was with the 10 percent I didn't agree with; whenever I tried writing about it, there was a pile-on. Most of them accused me of the same thing, that I was a spy who was there to "troll" the group and sow discontent.

And so my first and last membership in an online community came to a swift end, and I was left with a question. We all learn in school that we need to take an interest in social issues and that participation is crucial in a healthy democracy, but why, despite all the interest and participation, does it feel like the world is not getting better?

The problem isn't in how much we are participating but in how. When taking sides is prioritized over finding consensus, the discourse devolves into a purity test. Even when there is agreement on nine out of ten issues, the one disagreement renders the dissenter an impure element who needs to be removed. Rinse and repeat until only "our side" is left—the people who agree on all ten issues.

In the past, a family would gather around a television with only a handful of channels and go to school or work talking about the news or popular shows they had seen the evening before. But now, everyone gets their information from different sources. The YouTube algorithm shows you what you want to see, and the more extreme and one-sided the content, the more engagement it gets. Naturally, we have lost a sense of societal consensus, and our political landscape has become more fragmented than ever.

Which is why encountering someone who has different political opinions now feels like encountering an insane person. Other people seem ignorant and crude, or enemies to fight in a battle of good against evil. Korea, for example, is already divided into North and South; how much more fracturing can we take?

Not to mention that we're not exactly living in the Star Wars extended universe, where the divide between good and evil is a little more obvious. In *our* galaxy, evil is sometimes disguised as good, and good intentions don't always guarantee good results. In most organizations and individuals, good and evil coexist. The world is simply too complex to always come down on one side or the other.

But you can't really see that if you're preoccupied with taking sides all the time. Every little fault on the other side would look malicious, while a fault on your own side looks like a mere mistake or oversight. All of which would be only a distraction from dealing with the bigger issues at hand.

Often there is nothing more despicable than neutrality, but what are we to do? One of our greatest current hurdles is the side-taking. We need to rise above that to find common ground. Only then can we express our thoughts without ending up hating one another.

We need an alternative to this toxic mudslinging. We need persuasion over insults.

∧∧∧∧∧∧∧∧∧∧∧∧∧∧∧∧∧∧∧∧∧∧∧∧∧

ONLY WITH A NEUTRAL MINDSET CAN WE OVERCOME

THIS GIANT OBSTACLE OF CONFLICT BEFORE US

AND MOVE FORWARD INTO A BETTER FUTURE.

∧∧∧∧∧∧∧∧∧∧∧∧∧∧∧∧∧∧∧∧∧∧∧∧∧

Try looking at things from the other side.

☑ CREATE EVIDENCE FOR HOPE

I t's hard to talk about hope with a straight face these days. False hope can be toxic. Koreans have this thing called "hope torture" in which false hope is used to torture people into waiting for something that never comes.

The following is a somewhat problematic, if useful, example. There were many American prisoners of war (POWs) during the Vietnam War. Quite a few of them died because they couldn't endure incarceration, and according to Admiral James Stockdale, a former POW and US vice presidential candidate, the POWs who died earliest were the optimists. They believed they'd be released before Christmas, and when Christmas passed, Easter, and when Easter passed, Thanksgiving. By the next Christmas, they were dead. Was it hope that killed them? Not quite, because what they held on to wasn't hope but baseless optimism, which is more a form of escapism.

Would it be better to be a pessimist and not expect anything? That's not the answer, either. Because the next POWs to die were the pessimists. So what's the answer?

When he was a POW, Stockdale confronted reality and did what he could. He wounded himself by smashing his head against a chair so that the enemy couldn't film him for their propaganda about how well they treated POWs. He took back control however he could, creating an internal system of communication to decrease the sense of isolation among the prisoners. He wound up enduring seven years of POW life through the power of his own mind.

Korea once overflowed with optimists. They would predict upswings in the economy, and having read personal finance books, they became convinced they would soon strike it rich. But reality wasn't so prone to change. The childhood dictum that effort always pays off morphed into the dictum that effort only sometimes pays off, and our optimism often came back to us as disappointment. Thus, hope took its current place in our society as a tool for torture.

It's true: hope divorced from reality is just opium. But can we live without hope? We must hold on to it, albeit with our feet planted firmly in reality.

Just as one can't hope to lose weight by eating five large meals a day, you need to find a way to have hope if hope is what you want. Once you've thought it through, get ready for some disappointment along the way.

∧∧∧∧∧∧∧∧∧∧∧∧∧∧∧∧∧∧∧∧∧∧∧∧

WHAT YOU NEED TO DO IS NOT TO HOPE OR DESPAIR, BUT TO CREATE A FOUNDATION FOR HOPE.

∧∧∧∧∧∧∧∧∧∧∧∧∧∧∧∧∧∧∧∧∧∧∧∧

Hope for the best and prepare for the worst.
Where there's a will, there's a way.
The heavens help those who help themselves.
To catch a lion, you've got to enter the lion's den.

Hope is always conditional.

☑ BE GENEROUS

I tend to help a lot of strangers. I show senior citizens which subway to take, even writing down directions for them after looking it up on my phone. If I notice a woman being followed, I tell her she should take another route.

The reason I became so open to helping was because of my experience backpacking. I was able to finish my trip despite my phone breaking down and a language barrier and my unfamiliarity with my surroundings, all thanks to the kindness of strangers. In Korea, I don't face these challenges. I know how things work, I'm healthy, and I speak Korean.

I was unaware of how people without my privileges could use my help until I was in a situation in which I needed help.

My mother told me that I may come to regret helping strangers because they could hurt me. To her I say: when you're older, someone like me is going to help you.

If others repeatedly ignore you when you need help, you'll close your heart to them and stop asking for support. I don't want to live in a world where no one helps anyone else and we're all left to fend for ourselves.

What I need in life is care and concern, not distrust. I still believe that people are generally good.

^^^^^^^^^^^^^^^^^^^^^^^^^^^^

I WANT TO BE PROOF THAT THE WORLD STILL APPRECIATES GENEROSITY, AND I WANT TO HOLD ON TO THE BELIEF THAT IN MY HOUR OF NEED, SOMEONE WILL REACH OUT TO ME.

^^^^^^^^^^^^^^^^^^^^^^^^^^

Please pay forward the generosity you've received.

✓ DO NOT PARTICIPATE
IN THE HUNGER GAMES

A Hollywood actor's recent cheating scandal brought out many disbelieving fans who were quick to defend him. They didn't believe the story, not because they thought he was a paragon of virtue, but because *surely* he would never stoop to having sex with a nanny.

We may rage against discrimination and demand equality, but all too often that means only that *we* don't want to be looked down on—not that we shouldn't look down on others.

Just how discriminatory are we? I once made the mistake of looking at the comments section of a news article. One commenter proposed that the government could reduce youth unemployment by shutting down provincial universities that provide access to higher education for rural populations. Shocking enough that someone would say such a classist thing publicly, but even more shocking that this comment was upvoted to the top.

It made me think of the movie *The Hunger Games*, the dystopian story in which twenty-four "tributes" battle one another to the death. The fictional country's government devised this game to inspire fear, and went so far as to broadcast it live nationwide.

The game justifies killing twenty-three children by rewarding one winner with riches and fame. Players quickly form alliances and target the weakest ones for elimination first. This strategy allows the strongest to remain safe—for the time being. But only one will survive in the end, and just as the weak ones are eliminated, so are the strong. The story is an allegory of winner-take-all neoliberalism.

As in the movie, the stronger people in our society may briefly feel safe while the weakest get pushed off a cliff. But unless we stop pushing people off cliffs, no one is safe from being pushed themselves.

Some people say political change is the only path to a better world. We definitely need more transparency and fairness in politics. But to achieve this, we first must join together in solidarity and think more deeply about systemic issues.

We guarantee our safety not by trying to eliminate one another but by protecting one another. Enough with all the discrimination and competition.

∧∧∧∧∧∧∧∧∧∧∧∧∧∧∧∧∧∧∧∧∧∧∧

UNLESS YOU STOP PLAYING THE CRUEL COMPETITION GAME,

THE NEXT PERSON TO LOSE WILL BE YOU.

∧∧∧∧∧∧∧∧∧∧∧∧∧∧∧∧∧∧∧∧∧∧∧

HERE COMES A NEW GAME.

Please stop it.
Or everyone will die.

☑ DON'T BECOME A FAINT PERSON

I once took a two-day trip with a friend to a different region in Korea. We were passing a neighborhood I'd never been in and I looked up at the apartments and thought, *Those must be expensive.* How could I tell? That was simple enough. The buildings were new and near the center of town, and the apartment complex was built by a famous real estate brand. Just a few clues like that were enough for me to guess the price of the apartments.

A while ago I came across a viral posting titled "Class Predictor for the Republic of Korea." It divided up the Korean class system by income, assets, car make, college, hobbies, and other very granular details. We're already used to "silver spoon" and "dirt spoon" memes about class differences, but this posting was much more precise than that.

It did make me feel a bit sad. That ever since Adam and Eve were banished from Eden, society has always had haves and have-nots. Never have we been free from rank or class.

The problem with modern-day Korea, however, is that our societal problems are a little too obvious now. It's become a matter of resolution. Just as increased pixel count in an image makes it much clearer, our socioeconomic differences are also becoming harder to ignore as we become more informed. It's pretty easy to tell just how rich someone is and where we stand financially, leaving us with feelings of inferiority or the endless desire to climb the ranks of class.

But assets and cars and appearances are just external things. Our essence as people depends on our insides, not on how we look. And with all this judging of how people look on the outside, our insides suffer and grow weak. The psychiatrist Jung Hye-shin warns that the fainter we become as selves, the more prone we become to endangering our mental health.

The more we try to outdo one another in the appearance wars, and the more we try to live up to the scrutiny and expectations of others, the more we lose our own light and become sicker inside. Of course, we can never completely ignore how our differences are being thrown in ever sharper relief, but we really do need to make an effort to focus on our own selves as people. We have to become intimate with that unique part of ourselves that has nothing to do with economic class or social status.

LIKE EVERY GREAT PHILOSOPHER THROUGHOUT THE AGES HAS SAID, OUR ULTIMATE PURPOSE IS FOUND IN SHIFTING FOCUS FROM THE DISTRACTIONS THAT SURROUND US TO OUR TRUE SELVES INSIDE US.

That's . . . not what he's asking of you.

✓ ASK YOURSELF WHAT
IT MEANS TO BE HUMAN

I once read an article about an apartment complex staffer who had held against their will a group of children who had come into the complex's playground. She claimed that children playing in someone else's playground was a form of robbery, and she cursed out the children, called the police, and on top of that refused to apologize to the children's parents, saying her actions were justified.

This idea that a playground belongs only to the people who live around it and that any child from the outside who happens to play in it is trespassing— there's some room for disagreement here. But to call the police on children who were only playing, that's a different story. Why didn't this person pause to think about how that might hurt or even traumatize the children? The question isn't about what's legal. We have to ask ourselves a more fundamental question: What does it mean to be human?

Any grandiose talk of humanity is prone to be seen as naïve or even hypocritical. But can we really leave this question unasked? Can we ever be truly happy without knowing the answer, or at least searching for it?

I'm a person of many flaws. I'm far from being someone who makes the right choice every time, and there are days when I'm embarrassed by my behavior.

∧∧∧∧∧∧∧∧∧∧∧∧∧∧∧∧∧∧∧∧∧∧∧∧∧

REGARDLESS OF MY FLAWS, I WILL CONTINUE TO ASK MYSELF WHAT IT MEANS TO BE HUMAN AND NEVER FORGET THE VALUE OF IMPROVING, AND I WILL ALWAYS TRY TO FIND A WAY TO WORK WITH OTHERS.

∧∧∧∧∧∧∧∧∧∧∧∧∧∧∧∧∧∧∧∧∧∧∧∧∧

Because that's what being human means to me.

You can tell what kind of person someone is not by what they have but by what they're ashamed—or not ashamed—of.

☑ BECOME A LOST SOUL

In the movie *Dead Poets Society*, there's a character named Neil who grows up under immense pressure to become a doctor but happens to get cast as the lead in his high school's production of *A Midsummer Night's Dream*. Even though Neil is having the time of his life indulging his talent and interests, his father commands him to quit the play and concentrate on his studies or he'll take him out of school. Neil rages against this, but when he sees his mother's sad, desperate face, he acquiesces. Neil's own face falls, helplessness and despair writ clear in his eyes. The next night, he takes his own life using his father's pistol. When the life you're born into is unbearable, and the life you want is out of reach, despair is the only thing you have left.

The psychiatrist Kim Hyun Chul speaks of Hungary, Japan, and Korea as countries where "wandering is not allowed." There's another thing these three countries have in common: a high suicide rate.

We believe experimentation ruins one's life; it's a taboo. We even call wayward youth "lost." Going to college, finding a job, getting married, having children, buying a house—all of these need to be achieved on time, without a moment to wander or be lost. Otherwise, one faces a lifetime of criticism and social isolation, beginning with your disappointed parents.

Thanks to this, Korea now has the highest suicide rate and the lowest birth rate in the developed world. What these two statistics have in common is that they show how we've given up on life's two main imperatives—to survive and to reproduce—and how unlivable we think Korea is. Our society judges you according to whether you cycle through its prescribed stages on time—even the slightest delay in this arbitrary timetable can make you deathly anxious. We've experienced much harder times as a country, and there are many countries in much worse situations than ours—which may make us sound like we're complaining about nothing. What we're really afraid of isn't falling into poverty but becoming isolated and socially disrespected. It isn't economic indicators of well-being but the hypocrisies of our society that put us on edge and make us despair.

Many consider Northern European countries to be the happiest. But according to the author Leo Bormans, the happiness of Northern Europe is due not necessarily to high income or better welfare systems but to societal freedoms, trust, and a culture that respects different talents and interests.

Our country is the exact opposite. No freedoms, the same lifestyle forced on everyone, and no trust. How liberating it would be if we were respected for whatever life we live and whomever we choose to become.

The freedom to wander and explore and be generous with those who wander and explore is as crucial to happiness as a strong welfare system. This is not some academic theory but a key to happiness, perhaps the most important one.

∧∧∧∧∧∧∧∧∧∧∧∧∧∧∧∧∧∧∧∧∧∧∧∧

TOLERANCE AND GENEROSITY TOWARD ONE ANOTHER

ARE WHAT WILL LEAD US OUT OF UNHAPPINESS.

∧∧∧∧∧∧∧∧∧∧∧∧∧∧∧∧∧∧∧∧∧∧∧∧

Let's stop being unhappy together.

PART SIX

Checklist for
a Good and Meaningful Life

Happiness comes from the capacity
to feel deeply, to enjoy simply, to think
freely, to risk life, to be needed.

—STORM JAMESON

☑ DON'T MAKE HAPPINESS
YOUR LIFE'S PURPOSE

When I was in high school, we had to do a presentation called What Is Life's Purpose? I don't remember my answer to this question, but I do recall that many of my classmates did their presentations on happiness. Even as adults, I think most people would name happiness as their ultimate purpose in life.

But humans are not romantic creatures who are born to be happy. If we were put on Earth to be happy, why is only one of our primordial emotions of joy, anger, hate, sadness, and surprise a positive emotion? And we don't need to delve into the teachings of Buddha or Arthur Schopenhauer to prove that life isn't exactly a field of happy flowers.

Especially when people who promote such a purpose and pretend that a perfectly happy life is possible make unhappy people think they've failed at life. It's this attitude that encourages unhappy people to pretend to be happy and to suppress their sadness in unhealthy ways.

But sadness is natural. If you eliminate bathrooms in the Palace of Versailles just because they don't look nice, don't be surprised if people defecate in public and even, well, step in it from time to time.

It's better to be sad once in a while. Just as too many clear days can bring on drought, we need the rains of sadness for the sake of our personal growth. We should try to be happy, of course, and I sincerely wish for your happiness. But the purpose of life will always be life itself, not happiness.

+

Someone who is happy six or seven out of ten times can be called a happy person. But someone who tries to be happy ten out of ten times? Just obsessed.

If we were truly as happy as we appear, Earth would be Eden.

#proofofhappiness #sogoddamnhappy #happyevidence

☑ LIVE LIGHTLY

The first time I traveled on my own was on a monthlong backpacking trip, and I was so anxious about it that I overpacked. Three books and two kinds of curlers, even. By the third week, my exhaustion from dragging around my huge bag made me hate everything about traveling. As I sat in the airport waiting for my next flight, I repacked my bag with only the essentials and tossed everything else in the trash. Despite some worries that I'd need that stuff later on, my burden did become lighter—both literally and figuratively.

A friend I met on that trip had been traveling for a year and a half, and all she had was one backpack. She packed only the important stuff, and whatever else she needed she bought on location. If her clothes got worn out, she would buy something new and throw out her old clothes. According to her, this is part of the fun of travel. We may pack a lot because we're anxious about having everything we need, but in the end we don't really need that much. We might have to buy some necessities here and there, but this slight inconvenience is often preferable to having to lug around a heavy load.

Life is like a long trip. You've got to travel light so you don't exhaust yourself. If you want to feel lighter, look again at what you're carrying around and find the courage to throw some things away. This could be anything—from items you never used on your trip, to worries about things that haven't even happened, to desires that make life unnecessarily heavy, to shame when you haven't done anything wrong, to fraught relationships that only exhaust you.

∧∧∧∧∧∧∧∧∧∧∧∧∧∧∧∧∧∧∧∧∧∧∧∧∧

DUMP ALL OF IT. DOING SO WILL SET YOU FREE.

∧∧∧∧∧∧∧∧∧∧∧∧∧∧∧∧∧∧∧∧∧∧∧∧∧

✦

If you want to live freely, discard what you can live without.
                                    —*Leo Tolstoy*

Please discard what you don't need in the appropriate bin.

☑ ADD VARIETY TO YOUR LIFE

In the movie *Oldboy*, the character Lee Woo-jin locks Oh Dae-su in a cell and makes him eat only fried dumplings for fifteen years. Why did Woo-jin do that? He could've put Dae-su to work or occasionally given him steamed dumplings instead of fried ones. But a friend told me to imagine a hamster running in place on its wheel, living the same way in the same place for its whole life. Would such a hamster experience time? A life in which every day is the same would seem to pass by in a single moment. By locking Dae-su in the same daily regimen, Woo-jin stole fifteen years of his life.

In an essay titled "Long-Lifer," the poet and essayist Pi Chundeuk wrote, "A person who has lived from day to day like a machine can be eighty and still have had a very short life." To live the same way every day is to both disregard life's infinite possibilities and lose oneself. So go see the ocean on the weekends, take a different route home after work, meet new people, or do something you've never tried before. Let go of your routines and try to surprise yourself.

**THE BEST WAY TO LIVE A LONG LIFE IS
NOT TO LIVE PAST EIGHTY BUT TO SEEK OUT
AS MANY NEW EXPERIENCES AS POSSIBLE.**

Change the algorithm of your life.

☑ TRY NOT TO BECOME A DRIED HUSK

I once went to a zoo in Australia when I was visiting a friend. As I marveled at the vastness and natural beauty of the grounds, a herd of what looked like Abercrombie & Fitch models walked past. In Korea, zoos are more for families with children, but in Australia, zoos are just another place for young people to hang out. An Australian I befriended on that trip told me her hobby was bird-watching. Literally, looking at birds. I realize that bird-watching is popular in a lot of places, but in Korea it's unheard of.

A Korean friend told me about an Australian teenager she knew who talked about how much he looked forward to Christmas and how much food his grandmother would make and how the whole family would gather and have a grand time.

I shouldn't generalize, but many Australians seem to enjoy being in nature and spending time with their families. Whereas Koreans spend our holidays with our family largely out of obligation, and Christmas is just a day to try not to feel sad and alone at home.

Our country was one of the poorest in the world by the end of the Korean War, and as a people we've made a collective decision to never look back and to keep moving forward. As a result, we've managed to achieve incredible economic growth in record time. The Korean title of the book *Korea: The Impossible Country* by Daniel Tudor translates literally as *Country of Miracles, Country of Lost Joy.* We do seem to have lost touch with everyday joys and pleasures for the sake of our economic miracle.

We've turned into dry husks in the midst of dehumanizing competition, where our emotions themselves have become labor to be endured. Because we're so desensitized, we seek greater and more immediate stimulation, and we've conditioned ourselves to accept drinking and consumerism as the end-all of pleasure. But after we've availed ourselves of these easy and expensive indulgences, our lives seem even more tedious, and we are left feeling even more bereft.

If you want to reconnect with the pleasures of life once more, try tuning in to the small joys in your front yard and appreciating the natural rhythms of life.

We need to learn, as early in life as possible, how to find pleasure in simple activities that don't cost a lot. This doesn't mean to be a cheapskate or live shabbily, but to find happiness in an easier way and at any time.

Find joy in your current, everyday life.

∧∧∧∧∧∧∧∧∧∧∧∧∧∧∧∧∧∧∧∧∧∧∧∧∧

NOW IS THE TIME TO USE YOUR CREATIVITY

AND IMAGINATION FOR YOUR BETTER WELL-BEING.

∧∧∧∧∧∧∧∧∧∧∧∧∧∧∧∧∧∧∧∧∧∧∧∧∧

☑ THE ONLY THING WITHIN YOUR CONTROL IS YOUR OWN HAPPINESS

My little sister was born more than a few years after I was. She was something of a final project for my parents. My mother always says that she'll be happy only once my sister has settled down in life. I'm sure all parents feel this way, but it's still sad to me. I want my mother to be happy on her own, for her happiness to be within her control, independent of my sister's happiness. Instead, it's as if she's placed her happiness outside her front door and is left to wait for someone to ring the doorbell so she can open the door and claim it.

And how does my sister feel about it? Her unhappiness becomes our parents' unhappiness. It's hard enough to find her own joy, but when she fails to do so, she feels guilty that her failure prevents our parents from being happy. When we constantly worry about one another's happiness, no one is happy.

How do we break this cycle? Even if the problem stems from our caring for one another, we ultimately have to accept the fact that each individual must take care of their own joy.

We often talk about making the ones we love happy, but unless you're some kind of emotional groundskeeper, you can never make sure anyone is always happy, and no one can make sure you're always happy. The happiness of others is outside of our control, and everyone is responsible for their own happiness. So don't neglect yours.

∧∧∧∧∧∧∧∧∧∧∧∧∧∧∧∧∧∧∧∧∧∧∧∧∧

AS MUCH AS WE LOVE AND CARE FOR ONE ANOTHER, ULTIMATELY WE'RE RESPONSIBLE FOR OUR OWN HAPPINESS. PLEASE BE HAPPY ON YOUR OWN.

∧∧∧∧∧∧∧∧∧∧∧∧∧∧∧∧∧∧∧∧∧∧∧∧∧

I worked hard, overcame difficulties,
and lived by my conscience.
I have the right to happiness.
We all do.

☑ THINK ABOUT WHAT YOU HAVE GAINED

Sometimes I come across people who are unhappy at whatever job they happen to be in. Their boss is a mess, or they're underpaid, or there's no future in that company—their litany of excuses is endless.

They seem to dream of a paradise, but unfortunately, there's no such thing as a perfect job—one in which you're needed, have fun, have a reasonable boss, are compensated well, and see a path for the future.

We make most of our choices from a limited selection. We can't shop for a life like we would shop at a big-box store. More important than the answer to the question "What am I gaining from this?" is the answer to the question "What am I willing to give up?"

Because you often have to determine which is the lesser of two evils: a lower salary or a strict boss, a gap in your résumé or less time with your child, not doing the work you want to do or not having a steady paycheck.

And thinking in the other extreme of only what you'll lose will mire you in regret. Because if you're not willing to give up anything, you'll never gain anything, either.

It makes me anxious, but because I chose it, I have no regrets.

☑ SAY GOODBYE TO THE PAST

My second-grade teacher had pet students whom she always called on in class and doted on. It made me feel like an extra in someone else's movie. How obvious her favoritism must've been if I noticed it even as a kid.

Later on, I learned that that teacher was notorious for accepting bribes. She once called my mother in for a conference, and when my mother showed up empty-handed, the teacher berated her. I guess there was a reason for her bias. But back then, I didn't know adults could be evil like that. I just thought, *I guess she doesn't like me*, and that sadness remained with me for a long time.

There are so many garbage people in this world. They hurt us as children and sometimes the wounds don't heal even once we're adults. It's understandable to point to these garbage people from our past when looking for the origins of our current problems. We don't have confidence because of our second-grade teacher or we lack self-esteem because of how our parents raised us or we suffer from feelings of inferiority because we were bullied.

Fine. But the reason we look to the past to diagnose the present is not because we want to receive some belated compensation for our traumatic experiences or because we're drama queens who want attention; it's because we want to sever the chain of causation and move on.

There are many pathetic and awkward and immature people, and it's inevitable you'll meet them. The truth I discovered in my past is that my teacher was just a pathetic human being, and my parents were just awkward and inexperienced, and my bullies were just immature. I had simply been too young to see these truths for what they were.

But we are no longer children, and we have earned the right to move on.

^^^^^^^^^^^^^^^^^^^^^^^^^

IF YOU DON'T WANT TO LIVE IN THE PAST, COMFORT THE FRAGILE PERSON YOU ONCE WERE AND BID FAREWELL TO THOSE WHO WERE IMMATURE OR WHO NEVER WILL MATURE.

^^^^^^^^^^^^^^^^^^^^^^^^^

Embrace the you who lived through your past.

It's all right now.

☑ LEAVE A MARGIN OF ERROR

Graphic designers work at slightly larger than actual print size to leave room for possible trimming errors. Years of experience have taught us to build in tolerances.

Life, too, should be like this. Our life can never be as neat as we may want it to be. Sometimes we put enormous effort into things that turn out to be unimportant, and there are wasteful moments no matter how careful we are. Life never falls precisely into place, nor is it always efficient. Instead of chastising yourself or regretting your actions, it's better to leave yourself a margin of error, like budgeting a "scatterbrain fee" for mistakes.

The things we do aren't always the smartest, and sometimes being scatterbrained is part of the ride. Life can't always be superefficient. It's our first go at life—we need a little trial and error.

^^^^^^^^^^^^^^^^^^^^^^^^^^^^^^

OUR ACCEPTANCE OF INEFFICIENCIES AND MISTAKES

WILL MAKE US MORE GENEROUS AND MORE FREE.

^^^^^^^^^^^^^^^^^^^^^^^^^^^^^^

Make up for your wasted time
by living longer.

☑ ACCEPT YOURSELF

I once met a woman who was a career counselor for older people. Some of the people she helped were geniuses, but their lives were not as easy as one might think.

Many of them did not get good grades in school because they found the emphasis on rote memorization difficult. Thomas Edison himself had trouble accepting 1 + 1 = 2. These are the kinds of people who often can't find a job where their genius is appreciated; they find "normal" jobs unbearable to the point that they have to take antidepressants to function at work.

People tell them, "Not everyone gets to do the work that they want to" or "Everyone else suffers as much as you do, you're hardly alone in that." This only brings on more guilt and self-recrimination. It makes them think, *Everyone else is doing fine, so why is life so hard for me?* We don't in fact all experience the same level of hardship. There are those who find dealing with others difficult, just like there are those who find running challenging. We're all different.

If you find something especially hard, it isn't because you're doing something wrong or you're quick to complain or you don't measure up—it's because it simply doesn't come easily for you. Just like it isn't your foot's fault if the very popular shoe you tried on doesn't fit well.

Don't chastise yourself if you find something difficult. What really makes it difficult is your lack of awareness of your own abilities and aptitudes. Attempting to understand yourself and seek help doesn't make you weak or incompetent.

It means you want to stop the torturous self-judgment and unnecessary guilt and accept yourself as you are.

To do that, what you need is to understand yourself and choose a way of life that actually suits you.

∧∧∧∧∧∧∧∧∧∧∧∧∧∧∧∧∧∧∧∧∧∧∧

**EVEN IF IT MEANS BEING MISUNDERSTOOD
FROM TIME TO TIME, YOU OWE IT TO YOURSELF
TO UNDERSTAND WHAT MAKES YOU YOU.**

∧∧∧∧∧∧∧∧∧∧∧∧∧∧∧∧∧∧∧∧∧∧∧

There's a Korean book titled *I Will Support You No Matter How You Live.*
But the support you need most is that which comes from yourself.
Tell that one person who will always be with you until the very last moment of your life:

I will support myself no matter how I live.

☑ TAKE AN INTEREST
IN YOUR OWN HAPPINESS

I once kept an "unhappiness notebook" in which I would record my feelings in moments of despair and reread my entries when I felt better. Doing so helped me realize how irrational and extreme my thinking was when I was depressed.

But having written in the notebook a few times, it only made me feel like I was unhappy all the time. I wound up changing the notebook to a "happiness notebook," in which I recorded how I felt in moments of happiness or when I had overcome despair.

These entries proved more helpful, enabling me to see how feelings of depression would eventually pass.

People say they want to be happy, but few make the effort to understand what actually makes them happy. Happiness isn't just served up on a silver platter; sometimes you have to figure it out.

There are so many things you can learn that make your life better, but more important than knowing your Myers-Briggs type or how to store different spices or do your taxes is knowing what makes you happy, what helps you recover from sadness, and what makes you feel alive—the know-how of happiness itself.

^^^^^^^^^^^^^^^^^^^^^^^^^^

**IF YOU WANT TO BE HAPPY, BECOME
INTERESTED IN WHAT MAKES YOU HAPPY.**

^^^^^^^^^^^^^^^^^^^^^^^^^^

☑️ **LOVE WHAT IS IMPERFECT**

 Professional go player Lee Sedol **VS** *AlphaGo*

 Analog watches **VS** *Digital watches*

 Handwritten letters **VS** *Email*

 Records **VS** *mp3s*

WE MAY IDEALIZE THE PERFECT,
BUT WE LOVE THE IMPERFECT.

☑ ASK YOURSELF HOW
YOU WANT TO LIVE

For a long time, I wondered whether life was meant to be enjoyed or to be a vehicle for the pursuit of meaning. It was hard to find a definitive answer.

To begin with, I didn't understand what it meant to find meaning in life. It all seemed so vague, an abstract idea divorced from reality. I gave up on this exhausting mission and decided instead to enjoy life, to live each moment with as much pleasure as possible. And for a while it was pretty good.

I focused on what many people consider the most important things in life, things that fit neatly into the major categories of work, relationships, pleasure, and physical and mental health. I refused to feel anxious about things that hadn't happened yet and found something I *wanted* to do that I *could* do and I *did* it. Want + can = do. I worked really hard to solve that equation.

It was fun and satisfying to see things fall into place. I met people along the way whom I could trust and who were on the same wavelength as I was; I distanced myself from those who were unimportant to me or unpleasant to be around; and I vowed never to pay attention to anyone who looked down on me.

I spent time pursuing pleasure in my life. I looked up at the sky several times a day to appreciate how beautiful it was. I confronted my problems and solved them. I strove to be healthy. My life became clearer and lighter the more I stepped away from the expectations of others.

But oddly enough, I kept wondering if I was living my life in the right way. It wasn't enough that I was being as true to myself as possible. I went back to the beginning and rethought my life's purpose. Its *meaning*.

What is it that makes life *meaningful*? After much thought, I concluded that it is about looking inward to discover your inner truth and goodness, and looking outward to realize this truth and goodness in the world. As Aristophanes said, "We need others to complete who we are." We find our meaning and values in our relationship with society and others.

This doesn't mean, of course, that we should sacrifice our whole lives in service of others. It means we should do what we can to understand our core values and try to embody them within the context of our society, creating our own place in society in the process.

In my case, I wanted the world to be a bit better than it was. I wanted a world in which poverty didn't necessarily make people spiral into despair. I wanted to make the world a little kinder. The reason I would offer our essential delivery workers something to drink when they came to my doorstep was because, small a gesture as it is, I wanted a world where we could still talk of generosity. I donated to causes for children and tried hard not to hurt others, and I want, with this book, to have at least a small impact on people's lives for the better.

People—myself included—will continue to ask the question of how to live. For now, my answer is to live a good life. To not overcomplicate things beyond that. To work hard and communicate well with loved ones, eat good food, listen to good music, read good books, and take in the sun on a nice day. The warmth of such days is perhaps all a good life is.

And, if possible, take a step toward a meaningful life. Discover the values that are most fundamental to yourself and try to grow into a better version of you. We may be nothing more than dust in this vast cosmos, but we can still overcome meaninglessness and preserve our dignity.

∧∧∧∧∧∧∧∧∧∧∧∧∧∧∧∧∧∧∧∧∧∧∧

REGARDLESS OF WHAT SOCIETY MAY CALL SUCCESS,

I WANT TO FEEL PRIDE IN MY LIFE.

∧∧∧∧∧∧∧∧∧∧∧∧∧∧∧∧∧∧∧∧∧∧∧

*True self-discovery is not trying to
make yourself into something special
but realizing you were already
special all along.*

☑ LIVE AS AN ADULT

When I was little, my mother seemed like the strongest person in the world. But in hindsight, she was just a woman in her thirties. The world must've been hard and scary for her, but she had to act like an adult for the sake of the people around her.

Now I'm an adult myself, and no one praises me for doing all the things that I used to be praised for as a kid, like eating well and sleeping well. I can't complain to my parents about not getting an allowance or else they'll reach for a straitjacket. It's not pleasant to think that I have to be an adult when I still want to be protected like a child, but at this age I can't just put on green tights and say I'm Peter Pan.

So you have to act like an adult, even if it's the most tedious thing ever, if only to keep putting food on the table. And if you keep acting like an adult, like our parents managed to do, you just might succeed in becoming one.

AFTERWORD

As an adult, I've realized that the world is a cold and cruel place. Its mores are completely absurd, and its people so judgmental that even the mediocre among us enjoy looking down on others. For a long time, I felt constant anxiety about my lack of a strong safety net and so I ignored my true desires for the sake of making a living.

But eventually I realized that I didn't want to become another cynical shadow slinking about in this cruel world.

So I thought about how I should live my life, and I asked myself lots of questions. What did I *really* need to feel shame about, and what was it absurd to be ashamed of? What were my deepest insecurities? What could possibly be gained from humiliation and discrimination? And why were so many people so unhappy?

In my search for answers, I realized that unhappiness and anxiety can come from social relationships, not just neurochemical imbalances in our minds. Aside from the anxiety related to survival, the distrust, hate, and sense of rivalry we feel toward others have infected the very air we breathe and made us feel shame about things we shouldn't be ashamed of, cowed by things we should not feel cowed by, and neurotically competitive in order to not be looked down upon.

In this state of constant tension, we become exhausted by blaming our-selves for things we haven't really been given a chance to think about. With this book, I wanted to say that all the anxiety and blame are unnec-essary. I wanted to extend support to those trapped in the lonely isola-tion of distrust, to signal to them that there are still people who yearn for a more human life.

In our cynical world, we have to learn to pay more attention to ourselves and those who are important to us. But we also have to fight injustice and cruelty if we are to hold on to our humanity and, for our own sake and that of others, do our part to build a better world.

For each of you, as you learn not to envy who you are not, to endure the cold gaze of the outside world, and to live as you are—I hope this book has made you feel a little more free to be yourself.

I wish us all good luck.

ACKNOWLEDGMENTS

I set out intending to write an easy-to-read social psychology book. Because I myself found sociology and social psychology books immensely consoling and illuminating, I figured others might find them helpful as well.

Of course, I was in a little over my head when I wrote it. There were days when all I did was pull my hair out, and sometimes I went hiking on the hill behind my house and screamed my head off.

There were so many other things I found difficult at the time, and for that I want to thank the me of 2016 for getting through them while still managing to write this book. I'd also like to reassure her that her talents seem just about enough for her not to completely ruin her life, so she should stop worrying about it.

To me this book is a manifesto and a promise to myself. I feel like I've managed to live up to it, and that I've internalized most of its principles. And I'm happy to report that I do feel healthier psychologically.

It is my modest yet sincere hope that I shall continue to give advice from a place of happiness, not as an unhappy writer telling others how to become happy or perpetuating a "cure" that ends up doing more harm than good.

I would like to thank the writers whose work became the seeds of my own. I would also like to thank my family, my friends, and my publishers for helping me to share my work with others.

Most of all, thank you to everyone who has read my book, especially those who are reading even these acknowledgments. I shall try to live as myself as much as possible. This seems to be the best way to repay my readers for all the love and support they have given me.

No matter where you are, and no matter what kind of life you live, I send you love and acceptance. Thank you for welcoming my work into your hands.

I wrote this book for you. Let's live as ourselves, together. See you again soon.

Your friend,

Kim Suhyun